Nuclear Playground

D1128082

LIBRARY
MAYVILLE STATE UNIVERSITY
MAYVILLE, ND 58257

South Sea Books

Robert C. Kiste
General Editor

Linley Chapman
Manuscript Editor

Everett A. Wingert
Associate Editor for Cartography

Editorial Board
Renée Heyum
David Hanlon
Alan Howard
Brij V. Lal
Norman Meller
Peter Pirie
Donald Topping
Deborah Waite

South Sea Books are published jointly by the University of Hawaii Press and the Pacific Islands Studies Program, Center for Asian and Pacific Studies, University of Hawaii. They include books of general interest that deal with the islands and peoples of the Pacific Ocean.

Nuclear Playground

Stewart Firth

South Sea Books
Pacific Islands Studies Program
Center for Asian and Pacific Studies
University of Hawaii

University of Hawaii Press
Honolulu

U
264
.F57
1987x

For Bill and Jan

© Stewart George Firth 1987
This book copyright under the Berne Convention.
No reproduction without permission. All rights reserved.

Published in North America by
University of Hawaii Press
2840 Kolowalu Street
Honolulu, Hawaii 96822

Simultaneously published in Australia by
Allen & Unwin Pty Ltd
8 Napier Street
North Sydney, NSW 2060
Australia

Library of Congress Catalog Card Number 87-050700
ISBN 0-8248-1144-5

Set in Palatino by Setrite Typesetters, Hong Kong
Printed by Dah Hua Printers, Hong Kong

LIBRARY
MAYVILLE STATE UNIVERSITY
MAYVILLE, ND 58257

Contents

Editor's Note

This volume is the second in a new series entitled *South Sea Books* published jointly by the University of Hawaii Press and the university's Pacific Islands Studies Program. The series includes works of general interest that deal with the peoples and islands of the Pacific Ocean.

The author of this volume, Dr. Stewart Firth, is a distinguished Australian scholar specializing in Pacific history. His home base is Macquarie University in Sydney, Australia, but he has also taught at the University of Hawaii. Dr. Firth's recent book *New Guinea under the Germans* has been quite well received. He has published many articles about Papua New Guinea history, and he regularly reviews books on Pacific politics and history for Australian newspapers.

With *Nuclear Playground*, Dr. Firth is venturing into new territory, and he is addressing issues that are of immense concern. Surprising as it may seem, after the nuclear destruction of Hiroshima and Nagasaki, the American public has by and large wanted to ignore the further development of nuclear weaponry. Firth calls us back to reality as he reviews the history of American, British, and French nuclear test programs in the Pacific. He pulls together a large range of data that have never been so assembled, and he writes with a distinct point of view. Appropriately, that view accurately reflects the concerns and fears of Pacific nations and peoples. Firth has done his homework well, and this volume is mandatory reading for anyone with an interest in the Pacific region.

ROBERT C. KISTE

Acknowledgements

This book represents part of the outcome of a research project generously funded since 1984 by the Australian Research Grants Scheme and Macquarie University.

I owe much to many people for help. I would like to thank Geoff Adlide, Jim Anthony, Dirk Ballendorf, Roger Clark, Brian Cosgrove, Faith Doherty, Bill Fisher, Murray Goot, Renee Heyum, Fran Hezel, Stuart Inder, Giff Johnson, Peter Jones, Bernie Keldermans, Kathy Kesolei, Brij Lal, John Langmore, Leonard Mason, Norman Meller, Nancy Morris, Warren Osmond, Karen Peacock, Michelle Sheather, Suliana Siwatibau, Beverley Symons and Floyd Takeuchi. I greatly valued the comments of Maynard Davies, Jan Gammage, Bob Kiste, Dennis O'Rourke and Ellen Whelan on earlier versions of the book. Kathie Smith drew the maps. Helma Neumann not only typed the book with extraordinary skill and speed; she also offered endless encouragement. Without Bill Gammage the book would never have been finished; without John Iremonger, the publisher, it would never have been started. Beverley, Verity and Charles Firth cheerfully accepted my preoccupation with writing about the nuclear issue.

Note on spelling

I have used the most recent spellings of island names, which nevertheless appear in earlier forms in some quotations: Belau rather than Palau; Enewetak, not Eniwetok; Kosrae, not Kusaie; Moruroa, not Mururoa; Pohnpei, not Ponape; Ujelang, not Ujilang.

Note on currency

All dollars mentioned in the text are US dollars.

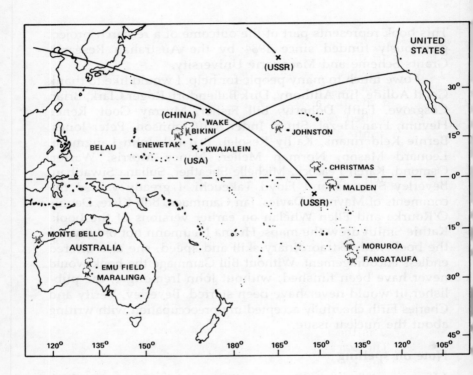

The nuclear Pacific, past and present, showing sites of nuclear bomb tests and major missile trajectories. The Americans and British tested until the early 1960s, leaving behind a radioactive legacy. The French still explode bombs at Moruroa Atoll. American, Soviet and Chinese missiles are fired to a variety of splashdown points in the Pacific.

Introduction

World War III could start in the Pacific. Long regarded by the USA as an American lake, the Pacific is now a focus of competition between the superpowers. With their great arc of bases from Alaska to Japan, Guam, the Philippines and Diego Garcia in the Indian Ocean, the Americans try to keep the Soviets bottled up on the Pacific coast of the USSR, where narrow straits offer the only access to open ocean. But the Soviets now have a major new naval base at Cam Ranh Bay in Vietnam and are steadily adding to their military forces. This development has sparked a response from the other side. The Americans are determined not to be outdone. They are planning more urgently for war in the Pacific, adding to their own mighty arsenal in the region and taunting the Soviets with aggressive surveillance and military exercises. The Soviets do the same. Both superpowers have nuclear submarines, nuclear bombers and nuclear cruise missiles. Both maintain a web of command and control posts. The navies of both countries carry nuclear weapons. Strategists on both sides call for more weapons to keep the 'balance'.

What is the purpose of this extraordinarily risky nuclear rivalry? The war planners answer in words which are designed to keep us confused and powerless. They talk of 'theater nuclear exchange on terms favourable to war termination' and creating a 'viable and credible nuclear deterrent'. The true meaning is simple and horrifying: the superpowers have equipped themselves with bombs which will put an end to human history if they are used; and because the logic of nuclear deterrence is that a threat must never be empty, the superpowers seriously intend to push the nuclear button if necessary. The Pacific could be where they first do so. Of the five nuclear powers, three—the USA, the USSR and China—launch missiles into the Pacific for test purposes; two—the USA and Britain—used to explode nuclear bombs there but have long since stopped; and one, France, continues to test its nuclear bombs in one of its Pacific colonies. Pacific Islanders have long resented the use of their ocean as a nuclear playground. They now fear that it might become a nuclear battleground.

To go to the atolls of the Pacific or to the deserts of Australia is to be reminded that nowhere on earth is remote. These are the places where the Americans and the British exploded nuclear bombs, and, in the case of Moruroa Atoll in French Polynesia, where the French still do. The nuclear bomb men have always assumed that atolls and deserts are a long way from anywhere. But they are wrong. Nuclear explosions in the atmosphere, which occurred frequently in the Pacific Islands between 1946 and 1975, were global in effect. The winds and seas carried radioactive contamination over vast areas of that fragile ecosphere on which we all depend for our survival and which we call the earth. In preparing for war, we were poisoning our planet and going into battle against nature itself. The atmospheric tests, now stopped, were like a miniature rehearsal for nuclear war itself, a symbol of our inability to find refuge. The nuclear age, we discovered, had bound together the destinies of all humankind. For more than a decade now France has pounded Moruroa Atoll with nuclear explosions underground, assuring us, as the atmospheric testers used to assure us, that all is well. But we have grown sceptical. Too many military men have told too many lies for too long. Like radiation itself, stories about contamination leak out from Moruroa. And the French never answer the obvious question: if underground testing is so safe, why not do it in France?

Nowhere on earth is remote, but some places are better to be in than others. The men who decided to test nuclear bombs in the Pacific and Australia live in Washington and London and Paris, not in the Marshall Islands, the Tuamotu Archipelago of French Polynesia or the Great Victoria Desert of South Australia, the places chosen by those men for their explosions.

The nuclear atolls and deserts are the homelands of other people, who are few in number and whose wishes could be disregarded. The Americans moved some atoll dwellers to make way for the bombs, others they covered with radioactive fallout. The British did not even bother to move people from one of the islands where they tested hydrogen bombs, and in Australia they proceeded with nuclear tests knowing that the danger zone for local fallout had not been cleared of Aborigines. The French tested their atmospheric weapons on uninhabited atolls, and kindly went to the trouble of building fallout shelters for Islanders in the vicinity, all the time denying that a fallout problem existed. To the military authorities of all three nuclear powers, the peoples of the atolls and deserts either did not matter at all or did not matter much.

This book is in part about those peoples, the Bikinians, the Enewetakese, the Rongelapese, the Utirikese, the Tureians, the Pitjantjatjara and Yankunytjatjara, their names almost as unfamiliar to the outside world as the story they have to tell. Together numbering no more than a few thousand, they have already lived in what might be our common future. Thanks to the mushroom clouds, they have experienced a radioactive environment at first-hand. Coming from traditional cultures which bent nature only gently to human purposes, they know the inhuman violence which a far more powerful culture can unleash. We should take careful note of their experiences, which might one day be ours.

The nuclear men have used the Pacific as their playground for 40 years, and the Pacific Islanders have had enough. Not long ago the islands of the South Pacific were almost all colonial territories under the rule of the foreign powers— Britain, France, Australia, New Zealand and the USA; today almost all are independent island states, the main exceptions being the French territories in New Caledonia and French Polynesia. No longer under the thumb of colonial governors, Island leaders are free to say what they think, and they are uniformly opposed to French nuclear tests and to the dumping of nuclear waste in the Pacific Ocean. Many New Zealanders think the same way. They have strongly opposed French nuclear tests in the Pacific ever since they began in 1966, yet France continues to test, and even organised an act of state terrorism in New Zealand in 1985 in order to stop Greenpeace from sending the *Rainbow Warrior* to Moruroa.

Even in Australia, where the Pacific Islands seem further away, anti-nuclear feeling grows. The American bases make

Australia a nuclear target. Britain treated Australia as a colony when it exploded its bombs in the Monte Bello Islands off Western Australia and at Emu and Maralinga in South Australia in the 1950s and 1960s. Long after the event, Australians are beginning to realise that the British, though squeamish about exposing their own population to fallout, were happy to contaminate the colonials in the lost cause of proving that Britain was still a first-rate power.

This book tells the story of the nuclear men in the Pacific Islands and Australia, and of those they displaced and irradiated. But it is also about what people and governments have done in response. The people of Belau, an island group in the Pacific to the east of the Philippines, drew up the world's first nuclear free constitution in 1979. Belau is among the tiniest of countries. Its capital, Koror, is an untidy straggle of tropical buildings along a single road, with coconut palms behind. The visitor can see everything in town within ten minutes. For the past seven years this small island territory, which is under American control, has been a thorn in the side of US strategic planners because not enough of its people will vote to abolish the nuclear free provision in the constitution as the USA would like. The people of Belau have not forgotten the American nuclear bombs which exploded over other islands in Micronesia. As Belau shows, the nuclear history of the Pacific explains why anti-nuclear sentiment is so strong in the region today.

The New Zealand government has lost faith in nuclear weapons as a form of defence and now bars all nuclear-armed or -powered vessels from its ports. Its policy has caused a crisis in relations with the USA, and undermined ANZUS, the defence treaty between Australia, New Zealand and the USA. Acting together, Australia, New Zealand and the Island states have declared a South Pacific nuclear free zone in an attempt to end French testing. The nuclear issue has transformed the political landscape of the South Pacific since mid-1984, loosening the US grip on the area and making the French more unpopular than ever. In the debate about the security of the region, its nuclear past will not be forgotten. Nuclear bombs have done no good for the Pacific and Australia so far; they will do no good in the future.

1

Where to Test?

The USA emerged from the Second World War a military colossus. Nothing demonstrated more clearly the unprecedented power in the hands of the Americans than the dramatic and destructive manner in which they ended the war with Japan. Over 40 years later Hiroshima and Nagasaki, two cities destroyed within minutes on 6 and 9 August 1945, remain symbols of the nuclear devastation which no one wants repeated and yet everyone fears to be increasingly likely. The continuing suffering of the atomic bomb survivors and their children in Japan from cancer and mental disturbance is a reminder of what life would be like for people not immediately killed by nuclear hostilities.

The suffering caused by war has never been the first consideration of statesmen and their military advisers. Nor was it in the USA in 1945. Power was the message spelt out to the Americans by the first atomic explosion at Alamogordo in the New Mexico desert; an awesome power which could deliver unique benefits to its possessor. As James F. Byrnes, afterwards US Secretary of State, said in June 1945, the bomb 'would make Russia more manageable in Europe'.[1] Its value was proved by the speed with which the Japanese capitulated. And within a few weeks of the end of the war military leaders were planning to develop the bomb further. By the close of the year the US Joint Chiefs of Staff had accepted plans for atomic testing, and on 10 January 1946 President Harry Truman gave his approval for the tests to proceed. 'We should not under any circumstances throw away our gun', said Truman, 'until we are sure that the rest of the world can't arm against us.'[2]

The specifications for an American atomic test site called for a large, protected anchorage in a warm climate within 1600 kilometres of a B—29 US Air Force base, under American control and either uninhabited or with a small population who could be evacuated. Somewhere in the Pacific Islands which the Americans had so recently captured from the Japanese, lay the obvious location—the Marshall Islands. The commander of Joint Task Force One, the combined military organisation established for the tests, settled upon Bikini atoll in the northern part of the islands. Foreigners had used the Pacific for a variety of purposes since the coming of the Spanish colonisers to Guam in the seventeenth century: they had cut down the stands of sandalwood trees until almost none was left; harpooned the whales; fished the coral reefs for pearlshell and trepang; organised a vast industry of trading posts and plantations to exploit the coconut; forced, persuaded, cajoled and convinced thousands upon thousands of Pacific Islanders to toil for three years or more on plantations which grew copra, sugar, cotton, rubber and other tropical crops; employed others to dig in the phosphate mines; and, with great success, preached the Christian Gospel. In Hawaii and New Zealand, where the foreigners took the most land, they created settlements which overwhelmed the original inhabitants. By the twentieth century all the Pacific Islands had become dependencies of one sort or another of European and US colonial empires.

Between 1941, when the Japanese bombed Pearl Harbour, and 1945, when the Americans bombed Hiroshima, the foreigners fought a bloody war in the Pacific Islands, wreaking destruction on a scale never seen before in that part of the world. The idea of using the Pacific Islands for vital military experiments was, however, new. That idea was a product of the atom bomb itself, the revolutionary weapon which could destroy so much that it had to be tested a long way from where the testers and their families lived. 'Everything about the bomb', wrote Bernard Brodie in 1946, 'is overshadowed by the twin facts that it exists and that its destructive power is fantastically great.'[3] Because it existed, knowledge of it could not be abolished; because it created such a huge explosion, the Americans would test it far from their own shores. Remoteness, which had once served to insulate Bikini atoll from the

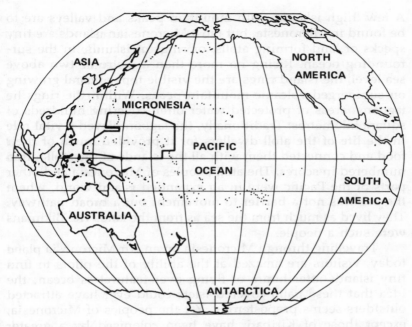

Micronesia, the last remaining UN Trust Territory, will be the only one not to gain full independence from the administering authority, in this case the USA.

rest of the world, now made it the centrepiece of American military attention.

To the people of Bikini, who numbered 166 in 1946, their atoll was not remote. It was home, the centre of all they knew. They lived in a part of the Pacific known to outsiders as Micronesia.

For convenience scholars divide the Pacific Islands into three culture areas: Melanesia, embracing New Guinea, the Solomons, Vanuatu, New Caledonia and perhaps Fiji; Polynesia, mostly contained within a broad triangle bounded by Hawaii, New Zealand and Easter Island but including other small island groups as well; and Micronesia, the islands and atolls dotted across the vast expanses of the Pacific from Belau in the west to the Mariana Islands in the north and the Gilbert Islands in the east. Of these three, Micronesia has the fewest people with the smallest land area and is the least well known.

A few 'high islands' with mountain peaks and valleys are to be found in Micronesia, but most Micronesian islands are tiny specks of land forming atolls, or rings of islands, in the surrounding ocean. Rising no more than a metre or two above sea level, the island rings are the visible tops of coral growing on submerged volcanic mountain peaks. Within the rings lie lagoons, areas of protected water often covering hundreds of square kilometres. Traditionally, the lagoon played a vital role in the life of the atoll dwellers for it provided much of their food and connected them with all the islands of the atoll, often numbered in scores. The atoll peoples of Micronesia and other parts of the Pacific were in an expanded island world, where the sea was not a barrier to movement but a broad pathway. They lived as much from the sea as from the land. The Bikinians were such a people.

Travelling through Micronesia on an Air Micronesia plane today, visitors are amazed at the ability of the pilots to find tiny islands after hours of flying over featureless ocean; the idea that these palm-covered islets could ever have attracted outsiders seems preposterous. Yet the peoples of Micronesia, except those of Kiribati, have been colonised by a greater number of foreign powers than any other Pacific Islanders. Within the space of 60 years from the 1880s the Islanders of the northern Marianas and the Carolines took orders from the Spanish, then the Germans, then the Japanese and finally the Americans. The Marshall Islanders had the same experience except that they missed out on the Spanish and got the Germans earlier. The islands of Micronesia changed hands again and again as part of a larger strategic game being played elsewhere, their people being too few and too divided to influence it. Copra and phosphate apart, the attractions of Micronesia to the colonial powers were not economic: they lay instead in its geopolitical position across the western Pacific just north of the equator. The Japanese, rulers from 1914 to 1944, fortified Micronesia using Truk lagoon in the Caroline Islands as their Pearl Harbour. The Americans, whose Naval Military Government replaced the Japanese in 1944, saw the region as vital to their strategic dominance of the western Pacific, and still do. They were determined not to let go of their recent Pacific conquests. While they considered how to keep Micronesia theirs, the Americans became the first nuclear colonisers of the Pacific Islands.

The atomic tests at Bikini on 1 and 25 July 1946, unlike any tests since, were conducted in the full glare of publicity. America wanted the world to know that it was strong. Pressmen and foreign observers came from everywhere. Photographers flew past the explosions, and published their pictures in popular magazines. Congressmen were there to watch the massive demonstration of American military strength. As planning proceeded *Operation Crossroads* developed into a giant festival of military and scientific curiosity. Competing interests in the military and scientific communities jostled for a high profile in the experiments. The Navy was there, and so was the Naval Air Force, the Army, the Army Air Force, the Naval Medical Research Bureau, together with teams of marine biologists, radiologists, oceanographers, physicists, chemists, geologists and even psychiatrists: 42 000 people, all of whom were men. The Americans recognised the unprecedented explosive power of the atom bomb but they continued to think of it as a weapon which would serve existing military strategies. As the author of the official history of the operation asked, why send tens of thousands of men across thousands of miles of ocean to observe 'two brief moments of majestic destruction?' And he replied: 'It was imperative to find how to improve our Navy. As long as we have a Navy—and we will have one as long as the possibility of war remains—we want to have one of highest possible quality. We want ships which are tough, even when threatened by atomic bombs; we want to keep the ships afloat, propellers turning, guns firing; we want to protect the crews so that, if fighting is necessary, they fight well today and return home unharmed tomorrow ... Which [of these two] stands up best to the terrific stresses imposed by atomic bombs: riveted seams or welded seams? ... Are the guns damaged? Do fuel supplies escape and burst into flames? Is ammunition set off?'[4]

The idea of building a nuclear-proof navy sounds bizarre in the 1980s, when eminent scientists predict that a general nuclear war would consign us all to a final, refrigerated morgue. As billions of tonnes of debris in the atmosphere shut out the warmth of the sun, temperatures would plummet to the point of extinguishing life itself. But in 1946 the Joint Chiefs of Staff thought atomic weapons belonged to the ordinary business of warfare in which men went on fighting after atomic explosions.

The lagoon at Bikini atoll is 40 kilometres long and 24 kilometres wide, and Bikini Island is the largest of 26 islands and islets which together cover a surface area of only seven square kilometres. Even in the preparations for the 1946 tests Bikini was changed almost beyond recognition. Navy men used bulldozers to sweep the area of the original village clear of vegetation; they built recreation areas and erected towers for photographic equipment, and they assembled a huge junk-yard of battleships, cruisers, destroyers, landing craft, floating dry docks, submarines and seaplanes in the lagoon at the point where the atomic bomb was to be detonated. The first test, *Able*, on 1 July, was seen by one observer in terms which became the symbol of the nuclear age: 'Then, suddenly we saw it—a huge column of clouds, dense, white, boiling up through the stratocumulus, looking much like any other thunderhead but climbing as no storm cloud ever could. The evil mushrooming head soon began to blossom out. It climbed rapidly to 30 000 or 40 000 feet, growing a tawny-pink from oxides of nitrogen, and seemed to be reaching out in an expanding umbrella overhead.'[5]

The second test, *Baker*, on 25 July, produced a gigantic column of water more than a kilometre high, lit from within by a burst of radioactive radiance. Men watching from 15 kilometres away, in fear and in awe, vomited at the sight. The explosion lifted the 26 000-ton battleship *Arkansas* on one end, and created waves 30 metres high. It produced intense levels of radioactivity in Bikini lagoon. Flying over the lagoon afterwards the men of the Radiological Safety Section noticed 'a burst of clicks, a crescendo, merging into the high-toned screaming of increasing radioactivity. The needle of one Geiger counter would rapidly go off scale; then the next, set to a less sensitive range, would follow suit'. As one of the radiologists commented, 'We are in the business of creating radiation out here—really fantastic amounts of radiation . . .'[6] The scientists at Bikini quickly understood the dangers created by introducing radioactive contamination into the interrelated biological systems of the lagoon and surrounding waters, and by

August 1946 a recommendation had been made that 'no fish, mollusk, or other marine animal taken within 100 miles of Bikini lagoon be used as food'. But naval commanders, trained in the arts of practicality and accustomed to believing in what they saw, found difficulty in accepting the idea of an invisible danger registered in the clicks on a scientist's machine. Sailors were put to work cleaning down decks with scrubbing brushes and buckets of soap and water, only to discover that the hardest scrubs made not one whit of difference to the levels of radioactivity being recorded by Geiger counters. The battered target ships were far more contaminated than had been expected. According to the official evaluation report, 'the second bomb threw large masses of highly radioactive water onto the decks and into the hulls of vessels. These contaminated ships became radioactive stoves, and would have burned all living things aboard them with invisible and painless but deadly radiation'.[7]

What conclusion was to be drawn from the Bikini tests? The potential of the atomic bomb to destroy directly and to kill in a lingering, insidious fashion had been confirmed beyond all doubt. A cautious scientific survey of Bikini in 1947 showed that, while radioactive material had been flushed from the waters of the lagoon into the open sea, the mud at the bottom remained 'highly radioactive'.[8] Whatever dangers the biologists might have seen, however, their opinions, like those of the scientific community at large, were not the decisive ones. Control of the atomic bomb belonged to the military men, with whom it would remain and who now wanted to make atomic weapons even more deadly.

The US Atomic Energy Commission, while not itself a military organisation, was set up primarily to serve military purposes. It was to develop atomic energy 'subject at all times to the paramount objective of assuring the common defense and security', and one of its first acts was to announce the establishment of a Pacific Proving Ground for the testing of atomic weapons.[9] Until 1962, when testing went underground, the Atomic Energy Commission organised 232 nuclear explosions in the atmosphere. Apart from a single test series in the Atlantic, all of these occurred in the Pacific Islands or at the Nevada Proving Ground, a site set up north-west of Las

Vegas in 1951 to specialise in experiments with small bombs up to the yield of the device which destroyed Hiroshima. The biggest and dirtiest bombs, those which created the most dangerous amounts of fallout, were detonated in the Pacific.

Enewetak, an atoll lying 350 kilometres west of Bikini, was chosen as the site of the Pacific Proving Ground. With a land area about the same as Bikini's, Enewetak encloses an elliptical lagoon 37 kilometres in diameter. The Americans were already familiar with Enewetak, having captured it from Japan in February 1944 in a bitter battle which cost the lives of 169 Americans and no fewer than 2661 Japanese.[10] The 1948 atomic tests consisted of three explosions from the tops of towers located on different islands of the atoll and conducted under conditions of secrecy. *Yoke, Zebra* and *X-Ray*, as the tests were called in the jargon of the military, were in the range of below 50 kilotons and left a legacy of bare ground and radioactive sand. The transformation of Enewetak did not truly begin until 1950 when the Americans embarked upon a massive program of constructing a permanent nuclear test site in the Pacific. Enewetak and Medren Islands, in the south-east of the atoll, became American towns in the middle of the ocean complete with recreation fields, barber shops, chapels, theatres and networks of residential streets with barracks and mess halls. Airstrips, wharves, laboratories, administration buildings and stores covered the remaining surface area of the islands. Anything less like the Enewetak of traditional times, with coconut palms and thatched houses, is hard to imagine. Here in urban Enewetak lived the scientists, engineers, construction workers and military men whose energies were directed towards the ultimate objective of producing bombs with greater capacity to destroy and kill.

President Truman announced early in 1950 that the USA would proceed with research into the development of 'the so-called hydrogen or super-bomb', a weapon drawing its power not from splitting atoms apart but from fusing them together. *Operation Greenhouse*, the test series at Enewetak in 1951, was designed to test the feasibility of such a weapon and on 1 November 1952 the Americans succeeded in crèating a thermonuclear or H—bomb explosion, the world's first. With a yield of 10.4 megatons, the blast was like 800 Hiroshimas all at once. It was detonated on Enewetak's northern side, on an islet which thereafter ceased to exist, leaving in its place a crater in the reef. The mushroom cloud shot upwards into the stratosphere at extraordinary speed. On the earth, life was snuffed out in a large radius encompassing neighbouring islands. For reasons which later mystified scientists, rats somehow survived on Enjebi Island, five kilometres from the centre point of the blast, but there was no doubt that this first H—bomb produced radiation problems 'of an entirely new order of magnitude'.[11] Men were playing God.

Meantime Britain became an atomic power, testing its first A—bomb just as the Americans fired their enormously more destructive H—bomb. In the affairs of states, gratitude counts for nothing and national interest for everything. British research on atomic energy played a crucial role in initiating the Manhattan Project which produced the first atomic bomb in 1945. It was Britain which alerted the USA in 1941 to the possibility of building such a weapon. But when the war finished, the USA froze Britain out of further nuclear co-operation. The McMahon Act of 1946 prohibited the exchange of nuclear information between the two wartime allies, and the USA raced ahead to make itself, for a few years, the sole possessor of the bomb. The British soon decided to develop their own independent nuclear capability. Victors in the war against Nazi Germany, rulers of a colonial empire which still stretched around the globe, the British thought of themselves as a Great Power. Their self—image required that they have the bomb, since not to have it would be an admission of decline to second-class status. So in great secrecy the British Labour government embarked on a program of developing nuclear weapons early in 1947.

Where to test? For the British, Britain itself was self-evidently out of the question. After all, they lived there. A British lieutenant-colonel involved in the atomic tests pointed out in 1985 that even minor experiments in the remote parts of Scotland could not have been contemplated: 'I doubt if the people owning the estates in Scotland would look on that with very great favour. They are interested in pheasants and deer in Scotland.'[12] Australia, on the other hand, was a long way away and had vast spaces which were supposedly uninhabited; even better, its Prime Minister elected in 1949, Robert Menzies, was British to his bootheels and could be relied upon to treat any request for a test site as an immense favour bestowed upon his country. In a top secret message in September 1950, Britain asked Menzies 'whether the Australian Government would be prepared in principle to agree that the first United Kingdom atomic weapon should be tested in Australian territory'. Without consulting his Cabinet Menzies said yes.[13]

The whole atomic project, the Australian government boasted in 1955, was 'a striking example of inter-Commonwealth co-operation on the grand scale. England has the bomb and the know-how; we have the open spaces, much technical skill and great willingness to help the Motherland.'[14] For the sake of Britain, whose nuclear weapons did nothing for Australia's defence, Australia would willingly accept radioactive contamination. England had the bomb; Australia would have the fallout. The USA and later France needed colonies as places to explode the bomb, and people under colonial rule were powerless to stop them. Britain, however, did not need a colony. Instead, the British could rely upon the colonial mentality of Menzies and his ministers.

'Well done, Sir William,' said Winston Churchill in his telegram to Dr W. G. Penney, director of the British team, after the first British A—bomb successfully vaporised a Royal Navy frigate in the Monte Bello Islands off the coast of Western Australia in 1952.[15] Between then and 1963 the British exploded a further 11 atomic bombs in Australia, at Monte Bello and at two sites in South Australia, Emu and Maralinga. They also carried out almost 600 smaller experiments with nuclear materials, many involving high explosives and most causing radioactive contamination.

Not even loyal Australia could stomach exposure to fallout from H—bombs, so to explode these the British went, like the Americans, to the Pacific Islands. Britain decided to develop its own H—bomb in 1952, but it was not until May 1957 that the first one burst over the ocean near Malden Island in the mid-Pacific. The British task force detonated a further eight nuclear bombs there and at Christmas Island in 1957 and 1958, six H—bombs and two A—bombs. Named by Captain Cook when he spent Christmas Day there in 1777, Christmas Island was one of the most far-flung possessions of the fading British

Empire. Lying just near the equator in the northern Line Islands, it was annexed by the British in 1888 and incorporated into their Gilbert and Ellice Islands Colony in 1919. Lever Brothers had once planted thousands of coconut palms there, and an eccentric French priest from Fiji, Emmanuel Rougier, had run a plantation, employing about 300 Gilbertese workers, which still existed in the 1950s. The Gilbertese stayed on the island during most of the tests. Malden, about 600 kilometres away to the south, had been the home of a group of Polynesians in ancient times but was uninhabited.

The British have been so secretive that little is known about their H—bomb tests. The first three, it seems, failed to meet expectations. According to the journalist, Chapman Pincher, who went to Christmas Island in 1957, the official statements 'claimed that the three test explosions ... had been highly successful. In fact, as I was told secretly after returning to London, they had all been something of a flop. They were big blasts, as I had seen for myself, but the yield had proved very disappointing.'[16] One member of the British task force thought the subsequent tests were also 'a matter of string and chewing gum', done in haste and without adequate preparation or resources.[17]

Like the British, the French believed their nation could be great only with its own nuclear bombs and decided to explode them in a Pacific colony. From the end of the Second World War onwards the French, who got nothing in return for helping the Americans to develop the atomic bomb, resented the nuclear dominance of the USA in the West. By the time General Charles de Gaulle assumed power in France in 1958 the decision to go nuclear had already been taken and preparations were under way to test the first French atomic bomb. But it was de Gaulle who put the *force de frappe* or 'strike force' of nuclear-armed bombers at the centre of French defence policy. It was, he said, to ensure that 'others should not become masters of our own destiny that we, too, are in the process of endowing ourselves with nuclear weapons'.[18] He wanted to show that France did not depend on the USA for defence against the Soviet Union, and to assert French independence from both the superpowers.

The Partial Test Ban Treaty, signed by the USA, the Soviet

Union and the UK in 1963, banned the testing of nuclear bombs in the atmosphere. In that same year de Gaulle announced that France would test nuclear bombs in the atmosphere at a nuclear base to be established in French Polynesia. France had exploded atomic bombs in the Sahara Desert in the early 1960s at the Reganne Firing Ground, but when Algeria won its independence from the French in 1962 they were forced to move to another colony, this time to the South Pacific. Originally acquired in the nineteenth century, French Polynesia had been intermittently useful to France for its copra and phosphate and for giving the French their own 'Pacific paradise'. The artist Paul Gauguin went there to paint and make love to Tahitian girls, free from the bourgeois constraints that he hated. French and Chinese settlers came. Alongside the original Polynesians, a population of *demis* or mixed-race people emerged. But French Polynesia, the less important of France's two main Pacific colonies, was a backwater of the empire when de Gaulle made his announcement.

Of the five groups of islands which make up French Polynesia, the one to catch the interest of the French military was the Tuamotu Archipelago which forms a wide arc north and east of Tahiti. The Tuamotus are low coral islands, almost all atolls. For their nuclear tests the French chose two atolls in the south-east of the Tuamotus, Moruroa and Fangataufa, which are about 1250 kilometres from Tahiti. As a support base the French took over the populated atoll of Hao. They said that the population within a 1000 kilometre radius of the nuclear sites was 'barely 4200 inhabitants'.[19]

Why Moruroa and Fangataufa? A French Ambassador put it this way: 'The site, established in an archipelago under French sovereignty, is made up of two uninhabited atolls, which lie several hundred kilometres from inhabited areas (with the exception of the small island of Tureia, under French sovereignty, 100 kilometres from the explosion point, which has a few dozen inhabitants, and where the necessary shelters have been constructed). There is obviously no region in Europe which has the same characteristics.'[20] To make things even more convenient, Moruroa is the only atoll in the south-east Tuamotus that has a lagoon that ships can enter, and where the French are able to set up a naval port. The crux of the matter, though, lies in the phrase 'French sovereignty'. French Polynesia is a good place to explode bombs because it is an Overseas Territory of France and politically subordinated to the Mother Country. Whatever the thoughts of the local inhabitants might be about nuclear tests these could be ignored or, if necessary, suppressed.

In the nuclear history of the Pacific, colonies and bomb tests go together. The USA, the UK and France all chose Pacific Island colonies as the places best suited for the biggest mushroom clouds and the most fallout. As for Australia, the British could use it as a nuclear colony because the Australian government was so keen to please.

2

Bravo

The 10-megaton H−bomb explosion at Enewetak in November 1952, kept secret by the Americans at the time, represented a quantum leap in the destructive power of nuclear weapons. But it was not a true 'bomb'. Weighing 65 tons and larger than a two-storey house, the unwieldy device could never have been delivered to a target. Nine months later the USA detected the first Soviet H−bomb explosion. The race was now on between the superpowers to develop deliverable H−bombs. That meant more Russian testing in Siberia and more American testing in the Pacific Islands; and one of those tests, *Bravo*, was to alert the world for the first time to the danger of global radioactive fallout. When a nuclear bomb explodes, it creates such high temperatures that everything near it vaporises and is borne aloft in a huge, expanding fireball. But as the fireball rises, it cools, and the vaporised materials condense into particles of different shapes and sizes. The larger radioactive particles fall to the earth within minutes or hours as 'local fallout', but the smaller ones will be carried by winds around the world for weeks and months, leaving a fine deposit of 'global fallout'. Both the early atomic and hydrogen bomb tests created global fallout, but the radioactive effects of the H−bombs were so serious that they created serious alarm and led in the end to a ban on atmospheric testing by the superpowers. Global fallout endangered not just Pacific Islanders and Aboriginal people in faraway places, but the populations of America and Europe, where the decisions about testing were made.

The Americans had left Bikini atoll alone since the first

tests in 1946. For the 1954 H—bomb tests they went back to
Bikini as part of an expanded Pacific Proving Ground. Their
first explosion was code-named *Bravo* and was scheduled for
1 March 1954. The meteorologists had forecast safe winds,
although the US Atomic Energy Commission later admitted
that the forecast approached 'the limits of human ability which
the art at present allows'.[1] In other words, they did not know
for certain what would happen when the bomb went off. The
sun that morning appeared to rise in the west as well as the
east of the northern Marshall Islands. Japanese fishermen
aboard a small vessel called the *Fukuryu Maru* saw a brilliant
glow fill the western sky at daybreak, changing colour from
white and yellow to red and orange. Villagers on the atolls of
Rongelap and Ailinginae, stirring early in the morning, also
witnessed the unnatural dazzle of light. Over Bikini to the
west, *Bravo*, the largest of all American nuclear blasts before
or since, had just erupted into a mighty vision of hell, the
equivalent of one thousand Hiroshimas. A vast fireball kilometres wide was bringing death and vaporisation to every
living thing within its reach. When one experienced atomic
scientist saw the fireball, larger than any he had seen before,
'the terrifying thought flashed into his mind that it might
swallow up the whole world, and he asked himself, "Isn't that
fireball ever going to stop?"'[2]

A searing wind was expanding in every direction. The
wind, which could be felt a hundred kilometres away, came
from the initial shockwave of compressed air forced from the
centre of the blast at 3500 kilometres an hour. It flattened trees
on distant islands of the atoll and whipped up 30-metre waves
in the lagoon. As enormous quantities of seawater were vaporised and parts of the reef disappeared, hundreds of millions of
tonnes of sand, soil and coral shot upwards into the atmosphere in new chemical forms to become floating, radioactive
particles. Ten minutes after the blast the mushroom cloud was
more than 100 kilometres across, bigger than most major cities.
It stood 30 kilometres tall over Bikini and it was drifting east
towards the Japanese fishermen, the ships of the American
task force, US servicemen on Rongerik atoll and the people of
Rongelap, Utirik and other atolls in the area.

As the radioactive cloud began to deposit ash on the

ocean, the ships of the task force made a rapid exit to the south, their personnel safely below decks. The gritty white ash fell for five hours on the *Fukuryu Maru* but the 23 Japanese fishermen went on working, brushing off the flakes as they floated down. They had caught few tuna and decided to return to Japan. On Rongerik atoll, where 28 American servicemen were making meteorological and radiological observations, measuring instruments began to record rapid increases in radioactive levels. Soon after 2.00 pm 'the needle swept past the extremity of its scale at 100 milirads per hour' and the men sought refuge inside an aluminium building.[3] Even there, gamma radiation from *Bravo* was reaching organs within their bodies. By the afternoon of the following day aircraft had evacuated them.

Meantime a layer of radioactive white powder was rising to a level of 10 centimetres over the island of Rongelap. Children played in it and adults discussed what it was. Someone said the Americans might have dropped the powder to kill mosquitoes. An American radiological safety team visited Rongelap, finding it to be dangerously radioactive and warning the people not to drink the water, but the Task Force craft did not evacuate the small Rongelapese population of 82 until more than two days after the blast at Bikini.

Billiet Edmond, a Marshallese who was then a teacher at Rongelap, recalls the fog of fallout which blanketed the island that morning and shut out the sun by 10.00 am:

> At 11.30 the classes were dismissed and the students and
> I went out and were greeted by the powder-like particle
> as it began to fall on the land. It did not alarm the
> islanders whom I met on my way back home . . . As we
> [were] chatting and drinking our coffee, the snowlike
> object was continuously falling in an increasing amount.
> The once blended green and yellow leaves of our coconut
> trees, breadfruits, pandanus have been gradually taking
> on the white colour of the falling stuff . . .
>   The once innocent and unviolent ashes took effect on
> the islanders in a sudden and most suffering incident. An
> unusually irritating itching punished the islanders in a
> most agonizing situation. The grown-ups were too old to
> have cried, but the kids were violently crying, scratching
> and more scratching; kicking, twisting and rolling, but
> nothing more we could do. [sic][4]

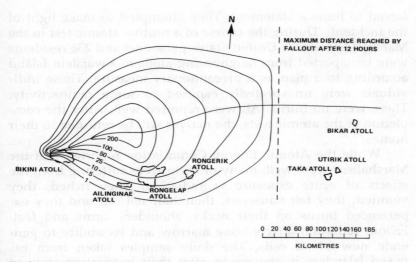

Radioactive fallout from the BRAVO H—bomb test at 6.45 pm on 1 March 1954. The gamma radiation is shown in roentgens received per hour, from 1 to 200. The safe limit for military personnel in the test series was no more than 3.9 roentgens over a period of 13 weeks. (Source: US Defense Nuclear Agency Castle Series 1954, p.219)

Still further east, the 157 Islanders of Utirik atoll, who witnessed a fine mist of fallout which began 22 hours after the *Bravo* shot, were also evacuated and taken to the American military installation at Kwajalein, the last exposed people not being moved until three days after the explosion. The task force considered evacuating the 400 people of Ailuk but decided that the dose of radiation they would receive from the fallout was safe.

Bravo created radioactive danger over a wide area. The USS *Patapsco*, a petrol tanker, was more than a thousand kilometres from Bikini en route to Honolulu when it was covered with the fallout on the afternoon of the day after the test. Men of the Pearl Harbor Naval Shipyard later decontaminated the vessel.

The US Atomic Energy Commission would have liked to maintain secrecy about what had happened at the *Bravo* test. But a serviceman in the task force wrote a letter about the fallout to a newspaper in Cincinnati, and the authorities were forced to issue a statement. They attempted to make light of the incident: 'During the course of a routine atomic test in the Marshall Islands, 28 United States personnel and 236 residents were transported from neighboring atolls to Kwajalein Island according to a plan as a precautionary measure. These individuals were unexpectedly exposed to some radioactivity. There were no burns. All were reported well. After the completion of the atomic tests, the natives will be returned to their homes.'[5]

While the Atomic Energy Commission reported that the Marshallese were well, many of them were suffering from the effects of acute exposure to radiation. They itched, they vomited, they felt nauseous, their hair fell out and they experienced burns on their necks, shoulders, arms and feet. Fallout radiation affects bone marrow and its ability to generate new blood cells. The daily samples taken from exposed Islanders in the weeks after their evacuation showed sharp falls in the number of certain blood cells, specifically granulocytes, leukocytes and neutrophiles.

In April 1954 the people of the Marshall Islands had an opportunity to tell the world what had happened. Like the other formerly Japanese islands of Micronesia, the Marshalls became a United Nations Trust Territory in 1947. Under the trusteeship agreement, the USA was in charge of the islands but had to report to the UN each year on its progress in administering them. Member countries of the UN Trusteeship Council could debate America's record as a colonial power, and the Pacific Islanders themselves had the right to petition the UN if they had grievances. A group of Marshallese sent such a petition to the UN, complaining about the radiation injuries inflicted by *Bravo* and asking that the US bomb tests 'be immediately ceased'. America now had to admit that, contrary to the first official statement, people had been hurt, but in the UN debate which followed in July the American representatives claimed that the exposed Islanders of Rongelap and Utirik had made a complete recovery. Looking confidently into the future, the US Atomic Energy Commission saw 'no reason to expect any permanent after-effects on the general health of these people'.[6] Events have since proved the Commission wrong.

The US Defense Nuclear Agency finally admitted in 1982 that 'Bravo was without question the worst single incident of fallout exposures in all the US atmospheric testing program'. According to the same source of information, the Bravo explosion was much bigger than expected and 'released large quantities of radioactive materials into the atmosphere, which were caught up in winds that spread the particles over a much larger area than anticipated. This resulted in the contamination and exposure of some individuals either stationed or residing on distant atolls or aboard various vessels. Acute radiation effects were observed among some of these people.'[7] Between 1954 and 1982 the official version changed markedly: a 'routine' nuclear test had become 'the worst single incident of fallout exposures'; 'no burns' had changed into 'acute radiation effects'. Like the British and later the French, the Americans constantly reassured people that they had nothing whatever to fear from nuclear tests.

People wonder whether even these admissions tell the whole story. Meteorologists at Bravo knew that winds up to 55000 feet were blowing in an easterly direction before the awesome device was detonated, yet, unbelievably, their superiors ordered that the explosion proceed. Unaware of the dangers of fallout and of the need to shelter from it, the Islanders should have been evacuated quickly. Instead, the Rongelap people had to wait two days and those of Utirik three days before American destroyers picked them up, whereas the American team on Rongerik was rescued one day after Bravo. Many Marshallese believe the delay was deliberate and that Bravo was meant to expose people to fallout so that the US Atomic Energy Commission would have a small irradiated population for long-term study. This belief is shared by a number of US Air Force weathermen who were on Rongerik Atoll during the test and who were interviewed by Australian filmmaker Dennis O'Rourke for his 1986 documentary on Bravo, 'Half Life'.

The facts seem to indicate a conspiracy by the US military to make the Islanders sick in order to gain scientific information about radiation effects. Not only was there foreknowledge of the wind direction, but the USS Gypsy, a destroyer, spent the day of the test at the entrance to Rongelap lagoon without evacuating the Islanders. Protecting themselves from the fallout, the Navy men measured the heavy doses of radiation being experienced by the unprotected and unsuspecting Islanders. They then sailed away, leaving the people of Rongelap to further contamination before they were finally picked up by USS *Philip* on the morning of 3 March. The Defense Nuclear Agency report on the 1954 atomic tests, released in 1982, makes no mention of the presence of the USS *Gypsy* at Rongelap.

On the other hand, sceptics have pointed out that the Joint Task Force Fleet, admittedly equipped with washdown equipment for a fallout emergency, was itself positioned directly in the path of the fallout east of Bikini and fled south as instruments began to record rapidly rising levels of radioactivity. Why, say the sceptics, would task force commanders have placed themselves and their men deliberately at risk? As for the delay in evacuating the Islanders, it might have arisen from the hesitations of men dealing with an unexpected situation: the official report depicts officers waiting for firm information about the fallout before deciding to evacuate people.

Controversy continues over exactly what happened in the northern Marshall Islands in the first three days of March 1954. The subject is politically sensitive for the Americans, especially in the Pacific. When 'Half Life' was shown to audiences in Papua New Guinea in 1986, the US Embassy in Port Moresby issued a lengthy statement. Embassy officials denied that America had conspired against the Islanders in 1954 and complained that the film failed to present the American perspective. O'Rourke, the filmmaker, countered by saying that the Marshallese reached the conclusion that they had been nuclear 'guinea pigs' long before he made 'Half Life'; all he had done was to let them speak, and to tell the story of the tragedy which now haunts them.

Two things about *Bravo* are indisputable: the Americans dealt with the problem of their own exposure to radiation before they bothered about the Islanders; and the fallout caused long-term injuries to the Marshallese people.

The Japanese fishermen, not the Pacific Islanders, were the ones who made *Bravo* an international scandal. When they reached Japan on 14 March, doctors quickly realised that they exhibited all the signs of having been exposed to radiation. The Japanese people, still living with the appalling human consequences of Hiroshima and Nagasaki, were outraged. Demonstrators took to the streets in protest against the USA. The Japanese government demanded an inquiry. And in a scare which bankrupted many small traders, people stopped buying fish from the Pacific for fear of radioactive poisoning.

The news from Japan drew leaders from all over the world to condemn the USA, and American and Soviet testing in general. Calling for a stop to testing, the Indian Prime Minister Jawaharlal Nehru pointed out that 'Asia and her peoples appear to be always nearer these occurrences and experiments'. The Indian Ambassador to the USA complained that Americans 'did not value coloured people's lives' as much as those of white people. Albert Einstein and Albert Schweitzer, perhaps the two most respected Europeans of their generation, appealed for an end to nuclear explosions. In Britain, the horror of *Bravo* brought into being a little-known organisation called the Golders Green Committee for the Abolition of Nuclear Weapons. It was to become the Campaign for Nuclear Disarmament or CND, the organisation that turned the bomb into a central issue in British politics in the early 1960s and again in the 1980s.

Opinion in the USA was divided. President Eisenhower, in an admission that was surprisingly close to the truth, said of *Bravo* that 'this time something must have happened that we have never experienced before, and must have surprised and astonished the scientists'. At a press conference the head of the Atomic Energy Commission, Lewis Strauss, let slip a fact which was familiar to him but still unknown to the public. An H—bomb, he said, could destroy a city, even New York. The media seized on what he had said and for the first time Americans became aware that nuclear weapons were able to destroy everything that mattered. From this people drew different conclusions. One editor found it difficult to see 'how anybody who is not a Communist agent can object to our manufacturing H—bombs and then testing them'. Others wanted the USA to immediately stop testing the doomsday weapons. Eisenhower responded by giving a qualified promise that the USA would not build bigger bombs, and he privately ordered his officials to investigate banning tests. His officials were against the idea. They said it was against America's national interest, and Eisenhower accepted their advice. But proposals for test bans were now politically acceptable, and were to be repeated in the years that followed.[8]

Meantime Japan organised a scientific expedition to the western Pacific to test the waters for radioactivity. It found widespread contamination over vast areas of ocean and a movement of radioactive substances through the food chains, as small fish ate plankton, larger fish ate smaller fish and so on. Then in September 1954 Aikichi Kuboyama, radio operator of the *Fukuryu Maru*, died. The Japanese government said he died from radiation sickness, but American officials insisted that the cause of death was jaundice and had nothing to do with *Bravo*. The USA finally admitted responsibility and paid compensation, but not before another wave of Japanese protest. In an appeal to the Council of Asian Jurists in Calcutta in January 1955, Kuboyama's widow made a plea: 'Aikichi died at 6.55 pm on September 23, 1954 leaving behind his three small children, aged parents, brothers and me. My husband cried with his last breath "no more atomic and hydrogen bombs!" I lost my husband because of the American death ashes . . .'[9]

Bravo, the test which went wrong, brought two nuclear secrets into the open. The first was that H—bombs were weapons of annihilation. The second was that they created fallout which fell with alarming consistency around the world on the populations of the nuclear powers as well as elsewhere. The US Atomic Energy Commission, trying to calm people's fears, eventually released a report about fallout early in 1955.[10] It conceded that local fallout from *Bravo* extended over a distance of 360 kilometres and that a similar bomb dropped on the USA would kill everyone downwind of the mushroom cloud for about 260 kilometres. But global fallout, said the Commission, brought only tiny risks which were worth taking for the sake of keeping the USA and the free world secure. Few found this report reassuring. The scientists could not agree with each other. One of them, Robert Oppenheimer, had played a vital role in developing the A—bomb, only to be the victim of a McCarthyist witchhunt after he opposed the

H—bomb. His security clearance was not renewed after 1954. He stressed how much scientists did not know about the effects of fallout. 'Physicists don't know,' he said in 1955, 'specialists in genetics don't know. Nobody knows, and we must take account of this ignorance.'[11]

American public opinion gradually swung against nuclear tests, as people pondered the effects of fallout on themselves and their children. The Democratic candidate in the US Presidential election of 1956, Adlai Stevenson, called for a ban on the testing of large bombs. News from abroad was of scientists and prime ministers and parliaments alarmed by fallout, especially after Britain said that it, too, was going to explode H—bombs. By 1957 a Gallup poll showed that 63 per cent of Americans favoured a test ban, a sharp rise from earlier years. The USA and the Soviet Union were now engaged in a propaganda battle over the test ban issue, making pro-posal and counter-proposal in attempts to win international sympathy.

The Soviet Union announced on 31 March 1958 that it would stop testing if all other nations did so. The Russians had just finished a series of tests, and knew that the Americans were about to start one. The USA, as the Russians calculated, was placed in the embarrassing position of embarking on a major new sequence of explosions at a time when fear of fallout was becoming universal. Aware that the Russians had achieved a propaganda victory, the Americans pushed for a meeting of experts from both sides to determine whether a test ban could be monitored. The Soviet Union agreed, and the experts began their discussions in Geneva in July 1958.

The US tests of 1958, code-named *Operation Hardtack*, went ahead nevertheless.[12] They brought a frenzy of military activity to the Marshall Islands. As many nuclear devices were exploded during *Hardtack* as in all previous US Pacific tests: 33 at Bikini and Enewetak atolls between April and August 1958, and a further two high-altitude bombs over Johnston Atoll, an American possession 1300 kilometres west-southwest of Hawaii. The mushroom cloud from *Oak*, an explosion of 8.9 megatons on 29 June, reached the stratosphere over Enewetak within two minutes and deposited fallout 250 kilometres to the south-west on Ujelang atoll. Ujelang was the new home of the Enewetak people, who had been required to move there by the Americans. Even in exile the Enewetakese were not free of the bomb.

The scientists meeting at Geneva made considerable progress on the question of detecting nuclear explosions. President Eisenhower was encouraged, and in any case he wanted to show the world that America was serious about controlling the nuclear menace. He offered to stop testing for a year if the Soviet Union did the same. The USA, Britain and the Soviet Union all hastened to explode bombs in September and October 1958 as Eisenhower's deadline, 31 October, approached. The Russians spread fallout from huge explosions in the Barents Sea, north of the Arctic Circle. The British detonated H—bombs and A—bombs at Christmas Island. The Americans tested in the Nevada desert and increased radiation levels in the air at Los Angeles by 120 times. But by early November all three nuclear powers had stopped testing, and for the next two and a half years the world enjoyed temporary relief. Except for France, the moratorium on testing was observed.

Distrust between the superpowers dogged efforts to reach a permanent agreement on nuclear tests. While talking, both sides prepared to test again. The Russians were the first to break the ban. They did so in dramatic fashion by exploding 50 bombs in the atmosphere in 1961. Measured by explosive force, the Soviet tests of that year were greater than all previous tests. They included a gigantic detonation of 57 megatons on 30 October, almost four times as powerful as *Bravo*. The American response was to resume testing underground and then to go back to the atmosphere and to the Pacific Islands in Operation *Dominic*, the test series of 1962.

Only four of the 40 *Dominic* bombs were exploded in Nevada and they were all small. The other 36 tests took place in the Pacific Islands, which once again had the honour of receiving the bulk of radioactive contamination. But this time the Americans had to take account of opinion in the UN, which was increasingly critical of the way they governed the Trust Territory of the Pacific Islands. Enewetak, lying within the Trust Territory, was the obvious choice for a test site because of its existing installations, but for the Americans to test there again would be to invite the charge that they were not fulfilling their responsibilities towards the Marshallese under the trusteeship agreement. So Enewetak was ruled out in favour of Johnston Atoll, American territory, and Christmas Island, which President Kennedy persuaded the British to make available.

To test their bombs at Christmas Island, the British had done things on the cheap. The men lived in a city, but it was built of tents which rotted in the tropical climate. Dysentery broke out because of unsanitary conditions. The first H—bombs did not go off as expected. The Americans came with 60 warships, 11 800 men, and the resources to transform Christmas into the home away from home which all US task force personnel expected. Most of the detonations in 1962 were of bombs dropped from aircraft, but five were high altitude explosions set off to discover their effect on communications and their potential for stopping incoming missiles. The highest, at 400 kilometres above the earth, was effectively a 1.4 megaton bomb exploded in space. It lit the sky from Hawaii to Australia and, against all the predictions of the experts, 'added significantly to the electrons in the Van Allen belts', a belt of charged particle clusters above the atmosphere. In the opinion of Glenn Seaborg, then chairman of the US Atomic Energy Commission, the consequences of this explosion 'should have a sobering effect on any who believe that the earth's outer environment could emerge from a full nuclear exchange without severe damage'.[13] The space blast put out street lights in Hawaii, 1300 kilometres away, by creating a sudden and violent electromagnetic pulse which caused surges of current in power cables. Many residents of Honolulu can still remember the event, which alerted scientists for the first time to the existence of the pulse effect.

The name given to the final US nuclear test in the Pacific conducted on 4 November 1962, was *Tightrope*. The Americans and Russians had walked a tightrope since the end of the Second World War, but during the Cuba crisis of October 1962 the rope suddenly jerked and threatened to send the superpowers and the rest of humanity tumbling to destruction. It was this crisis which produced the political will for a genuine agreement on nuclear tests. Frightened by what could have happened, Kennedy and Krushchev produced the Partial Test Ban Treaty of 1963, properly known as the Treaty Banning Nuclear Weapon Tests in the Atmosphere, in Outer Space and Under Water. That still left a place to test, under the surface of the earth, and Kennedy gained the support of the US armed forces by promising a program of underground testing which continues to this day. Ironically, the Partial Test Ban Treaty did nothing to disarm the superpowers but a great deal to disarm the peace movement, which was under the mistaken impression that the arms race had been checked. France tested in the atmosphere until 1974 and China did not renounce atmospheric testing until 1986.

Bravo had long-term consequences for nuclear politics. It sparked the concern about fallout which was to lead to a permanent ban on atmospheric testing by the USA, the Soviet Union and the UK. It made people realise the finality of nuclear war. And in the Pacific Islands, because of the injuries inflicted on people who were hardly noticed at the time, *Bravo* has become a symbol of the US debt to the Marshallese and, more generally, of the dangers posed to all Islanders by nuclear activities in the region. People all over the Pacific now mark Pacific Nuclear Free Day on 1 March, the date of the *Bravo* explosion. Just as the reaction against *Bravo* helped to inspire CND in Britain, so it has inspired the movement for a nuclear free and independent Pacific. More than 30 years later *Bravo* is not forgotten.

3

Unto the Promised Land

A gross disproportion of resources and military power between the Americans and the people of the Marshall Islands characterised the entire nuclear test program between 1946 and 1958. The Bikinians and Enewetakese did not ask to be moved from their home atolls to make way for the tests; they were moved. Had these Islanders been more numerous and powerful the Americans would have had to test elsewhere, but they were few and weak and had no choice but to co-operate with the men of the US Navy. The Bikini people, 166 in all, were the first to be relocated. When the military governor of the Marshalls arrived in February 1946, he compared the Bikinians with the children of Israel whom the Lord had led unto the Promised Land and explained that the atomic tests were 'for the good of mankind and to end all world wars'. After this assurance Chief Juda is reported as having said: 'If the US government and the scientists of the world want to use our island and atoll for furthering development, which with God's blessing will result in kindness and benefit to all mankind, my people will be pleased to go elsewhere.'[1]

Impressed by the evident technological superiority of the Americans, who had just defeated their former colonial masters the Japanese, and in the belief that their absence would be temporary, the people of Bikini agreed to leave. As a new home they chose the uninhabited atoll of Rongerik to the east. Briefly they were the focus of press attention in the USA, so much so that the final church service had to be repeated three times for the sake of newsreel cameramen. They left on a Navy vessel on 7 March 1946.

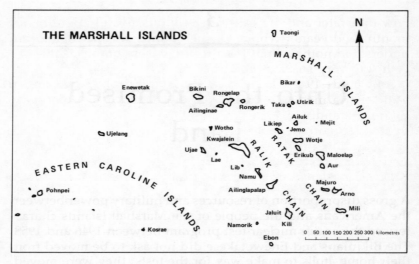

The Americans exploded 66 atomic and hydrogen bombs at Bikini and Enewetak atolls between 1946 and 1958, and continue to use Kwajalein atoll for testing ICBM's. Marshall Islanders were moved to make way for the tests and some were covered with radioactive fallout. The long-term consequences of the tests for the people of the northern Marshalls have been radiation illness, fear of the future and dependence on welfare handouts.

A Navy press release reported that the 'natives are delighted, enthusiastic about the atomic bomb, which already has brought them prosperity and a new promising future'. The new settlement on Rongerik, partly built by the Navy, was said to be 'a model village ... that anyone would be proud to live in'. In fact the move to Rongerik soon brought the Bikinians nothing but trouble: the atoll was smaller than Bikini; its lagoon held fewer fish; coconut palms and pandanus trees were less luxuriant; and food grew short. The people appealed to the American authorities to be allowed to go home. On a visit to Rongerik in September 1946 a group of scientists was asked by Chief Juda when the return would occur: 'It was no pleasant task to have to inform him that we thought it would be a long time yet. We tried to explain how the trees and the village had been pretty well destroyed and how the water and the fish were still unsafe and might be for months and years to come. Of such things, these people could understand nothing, but their feelings were unmistakable . . . "Oh, We very sorry to hear this".'[2]

By mid−1947 lack of food on Rongerik had become so acute that a medical officer reported malnutrition among the Bikinians, and when the anthropologist Leonard Mason went to Rongerik in January 1948 the community was in crisis. A doctor flown in soon afterwards said the people were starving. As an interim solution the Bikinians were evacuated to Kwajalein Island, an American military base to the south. Here they were accommodated in a village of tents and ate with Marshallese labourers in a mess hall. The experience brought the Bikinians into contact with the delights of the American way of life, 'movies, cokes, candy, ice cream'. Some members of the community, impressed by the egalitarianism of the Americans, began to question the authority of their paramount chief. When they voted in June 1948 on where to live the Bikinians chose an island in the far south of the Ralik chain, Kili, which was not the choice of their paramount chief and was beyond his jurisdiction.

Kili appeared to be a promising new home. In German and Japanese times it had been a copra plantation and it was covered with well-tended coconut palms. The soil was rich. But Kili also had notable drawbacks. It is a single island in the middle of the ocean, not part of an atoll. There is therefore no lagoon and the island is exposed to rough seas for at least half the year, during which time it is often cut off from the outside world. Fishing at Kili is no easy task, and the skills which the Bikinians possessed in lagoon fishing were of no use to them. At Bikini the Islanders had relieved the tedium of life by taking expeditions across the lagoon to other islands; on Kili no such trips were possible. As one man said: 'At Bikini, one could always go to another island, but here it's always the same. Sleep, wakeup, Kili. Sleep, wakeup, Kili. Again, sleep, wakeup, Kili.'[3] As on Rongerik food shortages occurred on Kili during the Bikinians' first year there. They longed for home, and many seem to have been determined that the resettlement should be a failure. They now blamed the USA for a great wrong and saw their best hope in appealing to the

Americans to look after them. Chiefs had traditionally cared for their people. An attitude of dependency has roots in Marshallese history. The Bikinians now transferred that attitude to an obviously wealthy and powerful patron, the United States.

For a few years in the 1950s the Bikinians seemed to be making a success of life in exile. They negotiated an agreement with the US government giving the Americans full use−rights to Bikini in return for $25 000 in cash which was distributed in 1956 among about 330 men, women and children, and a further $300 000 trust fund creating half-yearly interest payments. A development project gave the Bikinians a 17−metre schooner with an auxiliary engine to take their copra to Jaluit and return to Kili with supplies. And they gained access to extra land on nearby Jaluit atoll. But late in 1957 and early in 1958 two hurricanes tore through the southern Marshalls, sinking the Bikinians' boat and destroying their food and cash crops. Having almost achieved self-sufficiency, the Bikinians were once again thrown back on relief food, mainly rice and flour, from the Trust Territory administration. They never returned to self-sufficiency, seeing dependence on the obviously wealthy Americans as the best way to survive. The high birth rate, which increased the population from about 180 in 1948 to 300 by 1970, rendered Kili less and less satisfactory as a resource base.[4] As Juda, hereditary chief of Bikini, said in 1961: 'Our group of people here is getting larger every year and is increasing every year. It is difficult to take care of these people and the island is too small for them to live on. In a little while there will not be enough copra on the island to feed all the people ... Bikini is larger than Kili and we had plenty of land and a big lagoon. The Government moved us, therefore, it is up to the Government to find us a new place which is larger than Kili and better for the people.'[5]

The Bikinians continued to demand more compensation and a new home. On the basis of an extensive radiological survey of Bikini in 1967, the Atomic Energy Commission decided that the people could now live on their atoll safely, and in 1968 President Johnson announced that they would be repatriated. The Department of Defense and the Atomic Energy Commission undertook a quick clean-up of the atoll in 1969, dynamiting rusted towers, removing derelict vehicles, landing craft and machinery, filling holes and building roads around the main islands. The sixteen ships sent to the bottom of the lagoon by the 1946 atomic blasts stayed there.

Cleared of debris but still hot and bleak, the islands of Bikini and Eneu were replanted with coconut palms, bread-fruit and pandanus in the early 1970s, and by 1978 some 100 Bikinians had moved back to the atoll. The original view of the Atomic Energy Commission in 1969 that 'virtually no radiation' was left on Bikini proved false. While scientists argued about the long-term effects of low-level radiation, sur-veys began to indicate that all was not well. A radiological survey in 1975 found the interior of Bikini Island too radio-active for people to live there. The Bikinians asked for a more complete analysis and in 1977 the Lawrence Livermore Laboratory discovered dangerous concentrations of strontium-90 in well water. Because of radiation levels, the Bikinians were told they could eat only one coconut a day.[6] Tests on the people themselves showed that, through breathing and eating, they were absorbing levels of radioactive strontium and cesium which were considered to be unsafe over a long period. As a result, the American administration began supplying all food and water to the people from outside, so as to block the main pathways for the movement of radioactive materials into their bodies.

The 139 people on Bikini wanted to stay, but the US government decided in 1978 to move them off against their wishes because of the strontium and cesium they were in-gesting. An Interior Department official told a Congressional subcommittee that the atoll would be 'off limits for 30 to 50 years'. Government scientists said that the Bikinians might have taken into their bodies the largest dose of measurable radiation of any human population.[7]

The second evacuation of Bikini by the Bikinians took place in August 1978, when, carrying babies, bundles, suit-cases, and pandanus mats tied with string the people boarded the Trust Territory vessel *Micro-Pilot* on their way back to Kili. In the bureaucratic words of the Department of Energy, re-settlement of Bikini had 'suffered a setback due to radiation exposures significantly exceeding acceptable standards'.[8]

For the first time in almost 10 years, Bikinians went back to Bikini in July 1985. Led by the elected magistrate Tomaki Juda, Chief Juda's son, a delegation of 17 people inspected the atoll, island by island. The elder ones could identify fishing spots from the 1940s and the sites of the three islands vaporised in the nuclear tests. They travelled more than two kilometres across the *Bravo* underwater crater, which is 150 metres deep, an enduring reminder of the most infamous of all the American test shots. They observed the experiments being undertaken by scientists of the Lawrence Livermore Laboratory to determine ways of cleaning up Bikini, as the US government had by then promised to clean up the atoll. The scientists were trying to wash the radioactive soil with salt water, remove topsoil and apply potassium fertiliser in an attempt to lower the uptake of radioactive elements by coconut palms. How successful they will be, and how long it will be before Bikini is declared safe remains to be seen. Nor is it certain that the majority of Bikinians want to go back to Bikini, especially since the death of their leader Jibas Lejeto, who was vigorously in favour of the idea.[9]

Most Bikinians now live on Kili or at Kwajalein and Majuro, the urban centre of the Marshall Islands. Like many other Marshallese they have come to enjoy comfort, interest and variety as experienced in the more urban life of Majuro. Nevertheless, their constant aim since the 1950s has been to go back to their homeland and to obtain restitution for its loss. Bikini is not only a place that was lost but it is also the lever for gaining compensation from the US government now and in the future.

The US government revealed in 1978 that in addition to Bikini, Enewetak, Rongelap and Utirik, the 4 atolls whose contamination by fallout was publicly known, a further 10 'atolls or single islands' in the northern Marshalls 'received intermediate range fallout from one or more of the megaton range tests. A number of these atolls are presently inhabited while others are used for food collection.'[10] The atolls are Ailinginae, Ailuk, Bikar, Likiep, Rongerik, Taka, Ujelang and Wotho, and the isolated islands are Jemo and Mejit, both of which were dusted by fallout from *Bravo*. Since then thousands of people living in the area have filed lawsuits against the US government claiming compensation for personal injury, and an organisation representing the northern atolls has employed an independent scientist to make a comprehensive study of radiation levels.

Enewetak

The people of Enewetak atoll were also exiled by the Americans because of the nuclear tests. A few days before Christmas 1947, 142 Enewetakese disembarked from a US Navy landing craft at Ujelang atoll, the westernmost of all the Marshall Islands. An anthropologist reported that the people said: 'We did not give the Navy any trouble when they told us to leave Enewetak. We hated to go, but we obeyed. We want to co-operate with the Americans all of the time'. In traditional fashion, the Enewetakese did not make their feelings plain in a situation where they lacked power. According to a Navy report, they were 'happy and contented . . . practically every adult on the island took pains to approach the Civil Administrator and tell him "Good island"'.[11]

Ujelang is smaller than Enewetak and its resources were not always adequate to prevent hunger among the settlers. Deeply attached to their homeland, which by the early 1950s was populated by thousands of Americans, the Enewetak people never abandoned hope of returning. In the words of two of their chiefs: 'We do not like it as well as our home atoll, Enewetak. It is not as good a place to live. Ujilang is very much smaller, both in lagoon and land area. It does not have the large quantities of food that Enewetak provided, especially shellfish, particularly the large clams which were so important there. Nor does it have the large number of tuna, mackerel, and other fish. Ujilang does not provide anywhere near the numbers of turtles, porpoises, and seabirds, as did Enewetak, our old home. However, there is nothing we can do about it. We are weak and powerless, so why complain? So we will just try to do our best here on this small atoll.'[12]

The Enewetak people adjusted better to relocation than

the Bikinians. They had historical ties with Ujelang. Some traced their ancestry to earlier inhabitants of Ujelang and already knew the supernatural spirits of the atoll. For all its disadvantages of smallness and isolation, Ujelang was at least an atoll with 21 islands and a lagoon, a more familiar environment for atoll dwellers than Kili. Whereas the Bikinians were internally divided for years over questions of land use, the Enewetakese settled that vital issue soon after arriving in their new home and divided the new land along traditional lines; nor did they question the authority of their chiefs as the Bikinians did. Having moved to Ujelang, moreover, the Enewetak people stayed there; they were not taken from one island to another in a fruitless search for a place to live. Nevertheless, they looked back on their life in Enewetak as a golden age.

The Americans bowed to world opinion in using Johnston and Christmas Islands rather than Enewetak for the last Pacific nuclear tests. But they continued to use Enewetak as an impact area for missiles from California until 1968, leaving behind a wasteland littered with concrete and scrap metal. A rocket motor being tested in 1968 misfired, contaminating the southwest tip of Enjebi with radioactive beryllium. Two islands of the atoll disappeared during the 1950s. They were vaporised by nuclear explosions.[13] On others, topsoil and vegetation had been swept away in the tests, and regrowth was only of sparse scrub and grass. The atoll's south-east islands, where the Americans built their nuclear town in the Pacific, were virtually denuded of natural vegetation.

The Air Force Weapons Laboratory and the Defense Nuclear Agency began a new series of explosions on Enewetak in 1972. These were the Pacific Cratering Experiments or PACE, non-nuclear detonations designed to study existing nuclear craters and test the survivability of American missile silos. Once again, though on a much smaller scale, Enewetak atoll was being pounded by explosives. But this time the issue was far more politically sensitive. The people of Enewetak took legal action to restrain the Air Force from continuing with PACE and a federal judge in Hawaii granted an injunction to stop the experiments while public hearings were held.

The Air Force argued that Enewetak was the place to make the craters because the islands were already 'sorely ravaged products of the nuclear testing of the 1950s'. In its Environmental Impact Statement for the Enewetak people the Air Force said: 'The United States does not like war. There are governments who have atomic bombs, who could begin a war with us. Therefore, we are afraid for ourselves and our friends. We do not know how to keep ourselves safe from atomic bombs at this time. Our work in PACE will help us learn and, thus, will help keep us and our friends safe. We will use explosive shots to learn how big atomic bombs destroy things.'[14] To the surprise and chagrin of Air Force officials who went to Ujelang to explain PACE to the Enewetakese, the Islanders were all against the project and met the visiting delegations with signs saying 'PACE is bad'. The head of the community said:

> I do not know if you have made an attempt to compare your sense of values, you who live in America or elsewhere, with ours. You live with gold and money and we have to depend on land and whatever life we can find on land and in the water. Without these we are nothing. We do not have to explain further that Eniwetok, with whatever land resources and whatever marine resources it has, is our homeland, and seeing that you understand this, we do not know why you continue to insist to do these things on Eniwetok, when for us there is really nothing else to look forward to. For this reason we must continue to ask that you refrain from proceeding with this program. PACE is no good.
>
> Those of you here today have been to Eniwetok, as I have and some of our people have, and we all know that Eniwetok has undergone severe damage. There are islands that are missing, there is a considerable amount of land that has been destroyed. The question then comes: Has not Eniwetok done enough for your testing? We do not know who you will take this message to—perhaps you will take it to Washington or to the Department of Defense—but, the point still remains that we feel that Eniwetok has done enough. We have sacrificed enough and PACE should not be continued because it will only mean further damage and further destruction of our homeland.[15]

After further hearings in Honolulu the cratering experiments were discontinued. The Enewetak people had won a first victory against the US Department of Defense.

The desire of the Enewetakese people to return to their home atoll became more fervent over the years as the growing population on Ujelang, 340 by 1973, placed pressure on resources. More than once in the 1960s the people ran short of food, and in 1967 they demanded to be allowed to go to the district centre at Majuro to tell the government they were starving. When President Johnson announced in 1968 that the people of Bikini would be repatriated after their atoll was cleared of radiological debris the Enewetakese were spurred into vigorous protests, which the US Congress attempted to placate by awarding $1.02 million in compensation. Making use of legal aid the Enewetakese then succeeded in gaining a promise from the US government that it would give up Enewetak by 1974. Like Bikini, Enewetak was now to be cleaned up and made safe for human habitation.

The clean-up operation lasted from 1977 to 1980 and cost $100 million. Wearing paper masks to reduce contamination, soldiers and civilians had to remove thousands of cubic metres of radioactive scrap metal and concrete and over 100 000 cubic metres of radioactive soil, all of which was dumped in a nuclear crater on Runit Island and then capped with a huge concrete dome. Masses of other junk went to the bottom of the ocean.

The objective was to reduce the levels of dangerous radioactive isotopes at Enewetak: cesium−137, chemically similar to potassium, enters the food chain by travelling from the soil into fruits such as breadfruit and pandanus and then into the muscles of the body where it lodges, producing a risk of cancer; strontium−90 is also found in breadfruit and pandanus, and can cause leukemia; plutonium−239 enters the body mainly through the inhalation of contaminated dust; and cobalt−60 acts like strontium−90. No method exists of completely removing these residual radioactive materials from the environment. All that could be done was to reduce the hazards of living on Enewetak to what a Defense Department contractor called 'acceptable levels', while admitting that risks to health existed from long term exposure to low level radiation.[16]

Dilapidated buildings, towers, derelict boats, slabs of concrete, towers, antennas, sheet metal, pipes and cables were taken away. Tonnes of plutonium-contaminated topsoil were scraped from the surface. But in the end Enewetak remains the most radioactive ring of islands on earth apart from Bikini and Moruroa.

Traditionally, the Enewetakese consisted of two communities, one based on islands in the north-west and one in the south-east of the atoll. But the hopes of the northerners or 'people of Enjebi' that they would be able to return to their part of the atoll have been disappointed. Ten nuclear explosions took place on Enjebi Island and it is now too contaminated for people to live there. Even if the radioactive soil were successfully removed, radionuclides would still find their way into people's bodies through ground water.

So when about 500 people resettled on Enewetak in 1980, they were hardly going back to the homeland of their dreams. They could live on only three of the atoll's 40 islands, with only brief visits to other islands permitted; they would be monitored by scientists for radioactive intake; and Runit Island, with its vast concrete dome covering radioactive garbage, has been placed off-limits for ever. In a piece of extraordinary cheek, a US Army press officer called the Runit dome 'a monument to America's concern for humanity'.[17]

Atoll life in the Marshall Islands and elsewhere in the Pacific traditionally involved frequent trips across the lagoon to other islands to fish, collect birds' eggs, capture turtles or simply relieve tedium. Not only were such trips now restricted, but after more than 30 years away many people found readjustment to Enewetak impossible. For during that time away, the Enewetakese, like other Marshall Islanders, came to depend more and more on food given away by the US administration. About a hundred Islanders were back on Ujelang by March 1981 and another 130 moved permanently back to Ujelang in 1983.[18] The Enewetakese now live as two communities, one on Enewetak and one on Ujelang, where the trees which were planted provide a better living.

On Enewetak today, people depend almost entirely on food supplied under a US government program which began in 1980, and a delegation of Enewetakese told the UN Trusteeship Council in May 1985 that they would have to leave their

homeland a second time if the USA proceeded with plans to
stop food aid by 1986. Hertes John, one of the delegates, said
the free food would be needed for another three years.[19]

A question mark hangs over the future of the people who
live on Enewetak. To safeguard their health the Americans
have placed restrictions on living patterns: they may not grow
coconut palms on the north-west islands, for example, nor
may they eat coconut crabs (which absorb strontium—90) except from the southern islands. Yet these restrictions are not
enforceable. Some people, ignorant or foolhardy, might ignore
them. Even if the Enewetakese adhere to the restrictions, and
even if they do not receive doses of radiation excessive by
current standards, their doses might eventually become excessive by future standards.[20] Induced cancers and genetic
effects may not appear for decades.

4

'It turns out we were wrong'

In four trips during the last week of May 1985, the Greenpeace organization's vessel *Rainbow Warrior*, which was soon to be bombed by French secret service agents, evacuated the 300 people of Rongelap from their home atoll to Mejato, an uncontaminated island in Kwajalein atoll.[1] The evacuation coincided with meetings of the UN Trusteeship Council in New York, where the US Ambassador, Harvey Feldman, claimed that Rongelap received less radiation than Denver, Colorado, and that the islanders had been 'victimised by outside forces'. The leader of the Rongelap group, Jeton Anjain, said the evacuation had been instigated by him and his people, not by outsiders: 'We don't need the most brilliant scientists to come and tell us we are not sick. We know we have had health problems on Rongelap from the beginning—we are having them today and we will have them for the indefinite future. If the USA thinks that my people are okay why should they come twice a year to use them as guinea pigs? ... We have been suffering since 1954 and we are used to hardships. Our land is our most sacred possession but our children are more important than the land itself.'[2]

The Rongelap people, bringing dismantled houses, mats, suitcases and corrugated roofing, left their home because they were afraid of the effects of residual radiation deposited by fallout from the disastrous *Bravo* test of 1954 and from other American nuclear explosions in the northern Marshall Islands. Having lived for more than 30 years with the physical and psychological effects of exposure to radiation, not least being a fear of illness, the Islanders are determined to keep radiation risks to a minimum.

To begin with, the effects of fallout seemed to be temporary. People lost hair, felt nauseous and, because of radiation injury to bone marrow, the number of certain blood cells fell. Among children bloodcounts did not return to normal for more than two years. But the Islanders seemed to have regained their health. The people of Utirik, who were further from the blast, soon returned to their home island. Those of Rongelap lived for more than three years at Kwajalein atoll while scientists attempted to determine the extent of radioactive danger on Rongelap by examining soil, plants, fish, birds, clams and crabs for radioactive elements such as strontium—90. They found that strontium—90 generated by *Bravo* was being concentrated in the muscle and liver of the coconut crab and that, although fallout was heaviest at the northern end of the atoll, radioactive material was being distributed 'throughout the atoll' by the complex natural ecosystem.[3]

The Americans nevertheless decided that Rongelap was safe for human habitation again by 1957. According to one report: 'In spite of close confinement, the people appeared contented; they were going home. The trip was pleasant and uneventful, and the vessel arrived at Rongelap on the morning of 29 June 1957. Before debarking, all the Rongelapese gathered beneath the deck awning. There they offered prayers and hymns of thanksgiving to God for their safe return to their native land. The ship beached at 0900 hours that date. First object to be seen upon debarking was a huge canvas sign strung up between palm trees. In Marshallese it proclaimed, "Greetings, Rongelap people. We hope that your return to your atoll is a thing of joy and your hearts are happy."'[4]

The Rongelapese were in fact returning to an environment polluted by fallout not only from *Bravo* but also from the *Redwing* series of tests in 1956. The Islanders' body-burdens of cesium—137 increased by 60 times during the first year of return and those of strontium—90 by 20 times.[5] The American doctors who now made regular visits to Rongelap told the people not to eat coconut crabs, a Marshallese delicacy. The ban on eating crabs and the annual medical examinations by doctors of the Brookhaven National Laboratory became a source of continuing anxiety: if they were as healthy as the doctors said, people asked, why did they have to submit to repeated examinations?

The anxieties surfaced during a three-hour discussion with members of the UN Visiting Mission in March 1959. In a village which the Mission described as 'one of the cleanest and neatest seen anywhere in the Territory', the UN representatives nevertheless found a people 'gravely concerned with the effects of radiation on the atoll and in the lagoon which, they fear, has permanently contaminated coconut crabs and fish in the lagoon'. Numerous people complained about the contamination of fish, while others wanted to know the long-term outlook for their health.[6] The 1961 Visiting Mission was told of a variety of sicknesses among the Rongelapese, especially among children. People said miscarriages were now frequent and some children were being born deformed. They were 'seized by fear and anxiety', according to the UN representatives, who criticised the action of the Chief Justice of the Trust Territory in dismissing a civil suit for damages brought by the people of Rongelap against the USA in 1960.[7] Though the sample was small, the statistics certainly showed that Rongelap women exposed to fallout were having fewer pregnancies, fewer live births and more miscarriages than an unexposed control group. The people also told stories of horrifying stillbirths: a 'grape-like' mass; a baby with brains outside the skull; a baby which looked like an octopus.[8]

To examine the Rongelapese, the Atomic Energy Commission employed the Brookhaven National Laboratory, whose medical experts therefore had a financial incentive to depict the state of the Islanders' health in the most optimistic way. The experts were cautious. They did not think any long-term effects of exposure were likely 'in view of the small degree of irradiation suffered'.[9] But the experts were wrong. A twelve-year old Rongelap girl who was found to have a tumour on the thyroid in 1963 was only the first of many who developed the same condition. By 1979, 77 per cent of Rongelapese who were under 10 years of age in 1954 had been diagnosed as having thyroid tumours compared with 2.6 per cent in the unexposed control group. The effects of fallout even extended to babies in the womb: of three Rongelapese in their mothers' wombs at the time of *Bravo*, two have since been operated upon for the removal of thyroid nodules. Since 1965 the exposed people have had to take daily or weekly medication with L–thyroxine in an attempt to prevent the growth of

further nodules, and many have travelled to the United States
for thyroid operations. Even the conservative medical specialists of the Brookhaven National Laboratory now say that
tumours on the thyroid gland and, in some cases, stunted
growth are significant long-term effects of exposure to radiation
from fallout, and they predict that more tumours will appear
in the future.[10]

Lekoj Anjain, son of the former Rongelap Magistrate John
Anjain, had part of his thyroid removed in an operation in
1968. He was discharged with the injunction that he receive
thyroid hormone treatment for life. During the 1972 medical
survey he was found to have a low cell count in the blood and
later that year he died of leukemia at the National Cancer
Institute, Maryland, aged 19. He was one year old when the
fallout from *Bravo* covered Rongelap.

Whereas the experts employed by the US government are
prepared to concede only that Lekoj Anjain's death 'may have
been related to radiation exposure' the Rongelap people
have never doubted the connection.[11] The people now distrust the experts, whose earlier reassurances have proven false
and who are seen as being interested in the Islanders more as
objects of research than as human beings. The tone of the
early Brookhaven reports suggested that the doctors welcomed
the opportunity of studying a small, exposed population and
treated the needs of the people as secondary: 'The group of
irradiated Marshallese people offers a most valuable source of
data on human beings who have sustained injury from all the
possible modes of exposure . . .' and 'The habitation of these
people on Rongelap Islands affords the opportunity for a most
valuable ecological radiation study on human beings.'[12] The
visiting doctors carried out their annual examinations with
brisk efficiency and spent little time explaining things to the
people. Like many Pacific Islanders, the Rongelapese were co-
operative and agreeable in order to avoid giving offence, while
being privately resentful of their treatment.

The result was that even by the early 1970s few people
understood anything at all about radiation and its possible
consequences. In a letter to the head of the doctors' team in
1975, Nelson Anjain wrote: 'For me and the people on Rongelap,
it is life which matters most. For you it is facts and figures. We

want our life and our health. In all the years you've come to our island, you've never once treated us as people. You've never ... helped us honestly about our problems. You have told the people that the "worst is over", and then Lekoj Anjain died. I am very worried that we will suffer again and again.'[13]

The people of Utirik were told that the radiation dose they received from *Bravo* was too small to cause harm. But in 1976 they too suddenly exhibited a high incidence of thyroid tumours, a development unpredicted by the official team of doctors. 'It turns out we were wrong,' said Dr Robert Conard, head of the team, 'but we did it in all sincerity and I'm afraid the people have held that against me somewhat.'[14]

Dr Conard's attitude was illustrated in comments he made in 1969 after being asked by the people of Utirik why they had received nothing for having been exposed to fallout: 'I suppose we made a mistake in not giving the Utirik people a token payment and perhaps it is not too late to do something about it. Perhaps if we could give each exposed person $100 (including the descendant of deceased); I believe this would quiet their dissatisfaction. These people are very poor and even a very small amount of money would look big to them. Though we have managed to maintain fairly good rapport with these people, such a token payment would probably greatly improve the relationship. The 157 Utirik people so recompensed would not be a large sum of money.'[15] When the Atomic Energy Commission offered the Utirik people $100 each in 1971 they refused the money, saying it was not enough, though they later accepted a somewhat larger amount on the explicit understanding that no liability was being waived by the Americans.

Health and compensation

The effects of radiation on the health of the Marshallese today are fiercely disputed. Speaking to the Sixth Assembly of the World Council of Churches in Canada in 1983 the Marshallese public health worker Darlene Keju-Johnson said that the illnesses caused by fallout in her country were 'virtually endless' and included 'many cases of thyroid cancer, leukemia, cataracts,

miscarriages and stillbirths'. She described monsters born to
Marshallese women as 'jelly fish': 'The baby is born on the
labour table, and it breathes and moves up and down, but it is
not shaped like a human being. It looks like a bag of jelly.
These babies only live for a few hours. Sometimes, babies are
born with growths like horns on their heads, while others
have six fingers or toes'. The official US response was highly
critical of this claim and others like it. President Reagan's
Personal Representative for Micronesian Status Negotiations,
Fred M. Zeder II, condemned the remarks as 'the most naus-
eating example of bizarre propaganda I have ever seen'.[16]

The debate over radiation effects, charged with emotion,
will continue. On his visit to Australia in 1986 I talked to
Julian Riklon, the quietly-spoken Rongelap Islander who as-
sisted the *Rainbow Warrior* crew in moving his people to
a new home in 1985. He said he knew of monster births
from personal experience. Yet even sympathetic American
observers, such as the anthropologist Robert Kiste of the
University of Hawaii, a man who knows the Marshalls well,
doubt the truth of such stories. And US officials believe the
Marshallese overstate their case in order to gain leverage for
more compensation.

A few things can be said with certainty:

First, no one denies that fallout has caused high rates of
thyroid malignancies, extraordinarily high in the case of the
exposed people of Rongelap. Of all the internal organs of the
body, the thyroid is most susceptible to long-term damage
from radiation because it absorbs radioactive iodine. That is
why the Polish authorities hastened to treat children with an
iodine-potassium solution after the disastrous fire at the
Chernobyl nuclear reactor in the Soviet Union in 1986. Drawing
on knowledge gained from the sufferings of the Rongelap
Islanders, they sought to block the absorption of radioactivity
by children's thyroids and to prevent malignancies in the
future.

Second, the Americans' own studies of the 1950s showed
that fallout adversely affected the reproductive systems of
women. Exposed women at that time conceived less often
than expected, miscarried more often and gave birth to more
dead babies.

Third, fallout stunted the growth of some people, a condition related to thyroid illness.

Fourth, the knowledge that they have been exposed to some unseen poison has affected many people psychologically: not surprisingly they blame many illnesses on the bomb. As a woman of Utirik atoll said: 'The AEC [Atomic Energy Commission] doctors try to reassure us, but even now I am nauseous and very tired most of the time, and I know this is from the bomb. The AEC doctors tell us that this is unrelated to the poison. I now know that the poison will not go away from our islands.'[17] The Islanders' fear of an insidious poison is undeniably a major long-term effect of the atomic tests.

Final conclusions about the impact of the American tests on health cannot be reached for two reasons. No one yet knows how long it might take for illnesses to appear, though the direction of scientific thinking is not encouraging. Since the days when men of the US Navy tramped over the hot decks of the ships at Bikini as soon as the mushroom cloud had gone, or when marines jumped from trenches in the Nevada desert minutes after a nearby nuclear explosion, the safe threshold dose of radiation for human beings has been constantly revised downward to the point where scientists now say that no dose of ionising radiation, however small, is entirely without harmful effects. Of equal significance is the fact that US scientists have not monitored the health of any Marshallese other than those from Bikini, Enewetak, Utirik and Rongelap, even though the spread of fallout to other parts of the northern Marshalls has been officially admitted. According to Richard Gerry, Legal Counsel to the people of Rongelap, an independent medical survey in 1984 revealed 'many, many more thyroids which require attention and surgery' from other parts of the northern Marshalls.[18] The American doctors who examine the Rongelapese have not ruled out the possibility of genetic mutations in later generations. The effect of exposing sperm and ovum to ionising radiation might be seen also in grandchildren and great-grandchildren.

Yet it is a mistake to depict the situation of the Marshallese people solely in terms of their 'plight', as liberal commentators in the USA are apt to do. The Western tradition of seeing

Pacific Islanders as the denizens of a corrupted Paradise has a long history. It meets Western psychological needs. People in New York or Chicago or Sydney want to believe in the possibility of Paradise, an uncomplicated life free of tension and ambition such as Pacific Islanders are supposed to have led before Westerners intruded into their Garden of Eden. By this version of Pacific Islands culture, Islanders are simple folk who only want to be left alone; they are nothing but innocent victims of more powerful, worldly-wise outsiders.

Such a view of the Marshallese experience under the Americans is not totally wrong—the people dislocated and irradiated by atomic bomb tests in the 1950s are clearly innocent victims—but it is seriously misleading. Traditional Marshallese life was not free from tension or ambition, nor was it uncomplicated. In endless disputes over land Marshallese chiefs and their advisers mastered complex genealogical arguments to advance their cause, just as today Marshallese representatives are effective in presenting their case to the World Council of Churches, the US Congress and the UN Trusteeship Council. The Marshallese were using the foreign legal system of the Germans in land cases 80 years ago.

Today they have become adept at the litigation and politics of nuclear compensation. The Rongelapese attempted to bring a suit for damages against the US government as early as 1960. The Bikinians petitioned for compensation of $100 million in 1969 and soon afterwards began to use a legal aid organisation. Today all of the four 'nuclear atolls'—Bikini, Enewetak, Rongelap and Utirik—retain legal counsel and have large injury lawsuits before US courts, as do many other people from the northern Marshalls. In all, the claims are for more than $5 billion. Some American lawyers have a genuine interest in seeing justice done. Others, charging outrageous legal fees, are exploiting the Islanders.

To a large degree the nuclear issue in the Marshall Islands is now one of monetary compensation. People affected by the nuclear test programme regard the money so far paid or offered by the US government as quite inadequate to compensate for loss of land, damage to property and personal injury. From the beginning, the US government has been careful to avoid admitting legal liability. Its earliest payments, $325 000 for the

Bikinians and $175 000 for the Enewetakese in the 1950s, were lease moneys for the use of atolls. Congress voted $950 000 for the people of Rongelap in 1964 and since 1977 residents of Rongelap and Utirik who develop 'a defined radiation-related malignancy' have been eligible for $25 000 each. After a slow start, the Bikinians now have trust funds worth about $28 million, including money earmarked for resettlement purposes. But these are *ex gratia* payments. They reveal that the Americans accept moral responsibility for what has happened but not legal liability. Indeed the US government has consistently resisted nuclear claims by Pacific Islanders in court on the basis of 'what it regards as sound jurisdictional and substantive defenses', and it will continue to do so.[19]

In order to avoid the expenses it would face if the Marshallese damage suits were successful, the US government has produced a political settlement which is meant to stop all future nuclear claims by Islanders. Under the agreement an apparently generous compensation will be paid. A trust fund will generate about $270 million over the first 15 years of which $183.75 million will go to the 3000 or so people of the four atolls directly affected by the tests; $33 million to the Marshalls government for health care and monitoring radiation levels, and $53.25 million to a claims tribunal in the islands which will be able to compensate any individual Marshallese. The sting in the tail is that, as soon as the agreement comes into effect, Islanders will be barred from bringing nuclear cases before US courts. The agreement will be a 'full settlement of all claims, past, present and future'.[20] Existing lawsuits will be cancelled and no new ones permitted.

Giving testimony to a Congressional subcommittee in May 1984, Richard Gerry, for the Rongelap people, attacked this arrangement: 'We are dismayed that so basic a constitutional right as the right to sue should be denied people who have been victimized by US nuclear testing. If we were living under a totalitarian regime in which basic civil liberties were denied as part of the greater denial of human rights, we would expect to be barred from bringing suit against a negligent party. But we do not live in such a totalitarian regime. In fact, it is the United States that has taught the people of Micronesia about democratic freedoms and due process of law. How then can the United States, in good conscience, deny us access to judicial remedies for the atrocities which have been perpetrated upon innocent dependents under the provisions of the UN Charter?'[21]

The attempt by the USA to bar future lawsuits arising from its nuclear tests in the Pacific is now under challenge in the US Court of Claims, where the 1300 people of Bikini are suing the US government for hundreds of millions of dollars in compensation.

5

Staying while leaving

In January 1986 President Reagan signed legislation which will determine the future of the Marshallese and many other Micronesians. The measure approved a new political relationship between the USA and parts of its Micronesian colony, properly known as the Trust Territory of the Pacific Islands, which has been governed by the Americans since the Second World War. Under the new arrangements things are supposed to change for the Micronesians. They are supposed to be more in charge of their own destiny and less tied to what America wants. But a closer look at what has been happening in Washington suggests that in the future, as in the past, the USA will dominate Micronesia. US military requirements will, as always, come first and in many ways Micronesia will continue to be an American colony. The USA was able to test bombs in Micronesia because of the islands' colonial status; for a similar reason it will go on using the islands for military purposes.

Nowhere else in the world has the attempt to decolonise a territory taken so long or been so complicated as in the 2100 small islands and atolls of the US Trust Territory of the Pacific Islands. Negotiations over a new political status to replace the trusteeship, the drafting of constitutions, plebiscites in the islands and Congressional deliberations in Washington have now lasted for seventeen years. The UN has still not finally approved the termination of the trusteeship. Part of the trouble is the American political system, with its spacious provisions for Congress to amend treaties proposed by the executive branch of government, and the duplication of that system in the islands. But the fundamental reason why the decolonisation of Micronesia has taken so long is that the US government does not want it; nor do the majority of the Micronesians, if by decolonisation we mean the creation of either independent states or else self-governing states with a large measure of economic and political self-sufficiency. The USA wants to end the trusteeship because the charge that America is a colonial power is politically embarrassing. But the USA does not intend to surrender strategic control of the millions of square kilometres of the western Pacific encompassed by the Trust Territory. The form of decolonisation, designed for international consumption, must therefore differ from the substance which is continued American control. The attempt to hide substance behind form has inspired a succession of Byzantine formulations from Washington regarding the future of Micronesia's political status. America wants to stay in Micronesia while giving the appearance of leaving.

If this had not been the case the decolonisation of Micronesia would have occurred as swiftly as that of the other ten trusteeship territories. There would have been much less to negotiate: only the date of independence, the procedures for the transfer of power, and the nature of post-independence aid. As things have stood, however, trade-offs have been at the heart of a process of partial withdrawal by the colonial power. Alone among the trusteeship territories, Micronesia has not gained full political independence. The new political status of Micronesia will be 'free association' with the USA, a relationship without precedent in American history, and in many respects quite unlike the free association which the Cook Islands and Niue have with New Zealand. The agreement which determines this new, yet not so new, relationship between the USA and Micronesia is called the Compact of Free Association.

Why have the Americans never wanted to grant independence to their Trust Territory? Part of the answer lies in the American experience of war in the Pacific.

When the victorious Americans finally drove the Japanese from Micronesia in the latter half of 1944 they were determined that the islands on which so much American blood had been spilt should never change hands again. The war against Japan had demonstrated Micronesia's strategic significance to the

United States; it should stay firmly under American control. American memories of the war were filled with the names of Micronesian islands where bitter battles had been fought— Tarawa, Enewetak, Saipan, Tinian, Peleliu, Angaur. Altogether 7353 American troops died and 25 042 were wounded in the invasion of Japanese Micronesia.

American decision-makers were divided over the question of how to keep Micronesia under the Stars and Stripes. All agreed that the islands should not return to Japan, but the Navy and War Departments, together with the Joint Chiefs of Staff, wanted America to have exclusive control of Micronesia indefinitely. The military view was that the USA, having conquered the island territories of its enemy, should annex them. The Secretary of War Henry L. Stimson did not regard annexation as 'an attempt at colonialization or exploitation'. It was merely 'the acquisition by the USA of the necessary bases for the defense of the security of the Pacific for the future world. To serve such a purpose they must belong to the United States with absolute power to rule and fortify them. They are not colonies; they are outposts ... '[1]

The internationalists in Washington, well represented in the Departments of State and Interior, disagreed. In their opinion the USA could hardly preach anti-colonialism to the rest of the world at the same time as it annexed new territory. Micronesia, like other former German colonies, should be placed under the trusteeship system embodied in the UN Charter. At the beginning of 1946 President Truman decided that Micronesia should be a trusteeship territory under American administration.

The terms of the trusteeship remained to be defined, however, and on this question the military still had plenty to say. During 1946, as officials in Washington devised a trusteeship agreement, the Joint Chiefs of Staff laid down the conditions which they considered essential for American strategic interests. The result was a unique form of trusteeship which applied to Micronesia but to none of the other territories eventually placed under the international trusteeship system. It was the 'strategic trust', the effect of which was to permit the USA to close off areas of the Trust Territory for security reasons.[2]

The American draft of the agreement was discussed by

the UN Security Council early in 1947. The UN did accept one important amendment sponsored by the Soviet Union which was that the final agreement should provide for Micronesia to be like all the other trust territories and eventually achieve 'self-government or independence as may be appropriate to the particular circumstances of the trust territory and its peoples and the freely expressed wishes of the peoples concerned'.[3] The American draft referred only to the development of the territory towards self-government. While the USA conceded the theoretical possibility of independence for Micronesia, it has at no time since 1947 encouraged the Micronesians to become independent; on the contrary, American efforts have been consistently bent in the opposite direction of ensuring that the islands remain firmly tied to the USA. The reason for this is that the USA believes its strategic interests to be in danger unless the region is under American control of some kind.

The Micronesian trusteeship agreement is different from all the others in two other ways. Whereas trust territories such as Nauru, Western Samoa and New Guinea were under the jurisdiction of the UN General Assembly which approved the original agreements and passed resolutions to bring those agreements to an end at the point of independence, the Trust Territory of the Pacific Islands is under the jurisdiction of the UN Security Council. In addition, article 15 of the strategic trust agreement provides that it may not be 'altered, amended or terminated without the consent of the Administering Authority'. The purpose of these two unique arrangements was to ensure that the USA would have a double veto, both through its vote in the Security Council and through article 15, over any attempts by the UN to alter the trusteeship or bring it to an end. After a quick passage through Congress the agreement came into effect on 18 July 1947.

Strategy has remained the focus of US interest in Micronesia ever since. Speaking at a Congressional hearing in August 1984 Representative Beverly B. Byron of Maryland quoted the words of Mike Mansfield, who was a member of the House of Representatives when Congress authorised the trusteeship agreement in 1947. In that debate he said: 'We have no concealed motives because we want these islands for one purpose only, and that is national security. If it does become necessary to create a trusteeship for these islands, I would favor the proposals made by our State Department and President Truman which would place the mandates under the United Nations with the consideration that they should be catalogued as a strategic area outside the control of the Trusteeship Council.' The strategic importance of Micronesia, Byron added, 'has not lessened since Mr Mansfield made those comments'.[4]

America wants to keep the Soviet Union out of the western Pacific. For this reason the Department of Defense, the Office of the Secretary of Defense and the Office of the Joint Chiefs of Staff have all participated since 1969 in the negotiations over the Compact of Free Association. It could not have been drawn up without their approval. The Reagan Administration assured the Senate in 1982 that 'no decisions, major or minor' which affected the interests of the Department of Defense or the Joint Chiefs of Staff 'directly or indirectly, have been taken without DOD/JCS clearance or coordination'.[5] In a letter to Tip O'Neill, the Speaker of the US House of Representatives, on 24 July 1985, the then Commander of US forces in the Pacific, Admiral William J. Crowe, pointed to the strategic benefits for America in the Compact: 'From my point of view, the security aspects of the Compact are of great importance to our posture in the Pacific. The delegation of defense responsibilities and authority to the USA together with the provisions that the freely associated states will refrain from any action the USA determines to be inconsistent with defense and security requirements, provide the latitude needed to support our security interests. In addition, the Compact forecloses Micronesia to the military forces of third nations, guarantees our military forces unrestricted movement within Micronesia, and ensures continued access to the important missile testing facility at Kwajalein.'[6]

From the start the USA insisted on four strategic concessions by the Micronesians: the permanent denial of the islands to military use by any other country; unhindered transit by American military forces through Micronesia with whatever weapons they might be carrying, conventional or nuclear; the right to establish military bases on the islands in the future, either in areas already determined or elsewhere after consultation; and unhampered use of the Kwajalein Missile Range which plays a vital role in developing and testing America's long-range missiles. Under the 1986 Compact approved by Reagan, the USA has the right to Kwajalein for 15 years, with an option for a further 15 years.

The Americans have no doubts about the value of the Compact to their military interests. Democrat Morris Udall of Arizona and Chairman of the Committee on Interior and Insular Affairs told the House of Representatives in July 1985 that the Compact is an agreement 'which is very much in the interest of the United States'. It gives America, he said, the right of strategic denial, 'so that we are in a position for the rest of time to prevent any foreign power from establishing a military presence in Micronesia without our consent. That is an extraordinary concession made by the Micronesians and a very real achievement for the United States. It also gives us a 30-year lease agreement at the Kwajalein missile range, which is the single most important missile range we have in the entire world. Without the Compact, both the right of strategic denial and the lease on the Kwajalein missile range would be placed in jeopardy.'[7]

Republican John McCain of Arizona has put it even more strongly, saying that, in agreeing on the Compact, Americans have an opportunity 'from a strategic viewpoint to be on the brink of accomplishing something which eluded us in Vietnam, which eluded us in Iran, which seems to be eluding us in Nicaragua, and which may well have eluded us in the Philippines': a chance to act and not to react in defence of US national security.[8]

For their part, why have the majority of Micronesians been willing to settle for a political status which falls so far short of independence? There are a number of reasons. First, America is a superpower. The Micronesians number fewer than 150 000. Since independence has never been desired by the USA, the negotiator with power, it has never been a real option for the Micronesians. Second, their connection with the USA has given the Micronesians one of the highest per capita cash incomes in the Pacific Islands, together with access to welfare programs on a scale unmatched in the region. Accustomed to free school lunches, food aid and money to spend in supermarkets, many Micronesians are loath to go back to a standard of living which would truly reflect the meagre natural resources of their island environment. Without America they would be poor again. With America they can be relatively rich. And the lever for extracting resources from Washington has been the fact that America needs Micronesia strategically. As one observer has said, 'Micronesia's strategic importance is what pays the bills'.[9] The Micronesians have traded much of their sovereignty for a higher standard of living to be derived from payments under the Compact; and reflecting the basic logic of the deals which have been done, those parts of the Trust Territory which are worth more to the Americans in military terms will end up with more Compact money. In fact, the original Trust Territory has been split four ways since the mid-1970s as different groups of Islanders have attempted to maximise their bargaining strength. The people of the Northern Mariana Islands, still technically part of the Trust Territory, opted for US citizenship and Commonwealth status in 1975. Those islands have been effectively incorporated into the USA since 1976, and so the Compact does not apply to them.

The remainder of the territory was split in 1978 into three entities, each of which then drew up a constitution in preparation for self-government: in the west, the Republic of Palau, also known as Belau, with a population of about 15 000; in the east, the Republic of the Marshall Islands with 35 000 people; in between, the Federated States of Micronesia, encompassing Yap, Truk, Pohnpei and Kosrae states with a population of 84 000. Still parts of the Trust Territory administered by the USA, these 'republics' await emergence into the condition of semi-sovereignty which the UN Security Council alone can bestow.

The 'strategic trust' in Micronesia served America well for almost 40 years. It was a kind of military colony obtained with international approval through the UN. America exploded bombs there, closed off the Northern Mariana Islands for nine years so that the CIA could train anti-Communist agents from China and Tibet, and has fired experimental missiles into the region for a quarter of a century. The missiles will continue to come, and the USA is keeping open its options to build more military bases.

There is an irony in the American efforts to bring the

strategic trust to an end. In order to ensure that Micronesia was safely theirs, the Americans in the 1940s arranged for the Security Council of the UN rather than the Trusteeship Council to have the final say about the islands' political status. As article 83 of the UN Charter puts it, 'all functions of the United Nations relating to strategic areas, including the approval of the terms of the trusteeship agreements and of their alteration or amendment, shall be exercised by the Security Council'.[10] Only the Security Council can end the trusteeship agreement in a way which will be acceptable to the international community and the USA itself accepts that fact. The State Department has said that the Compact of Free Association will not enter into force until the UN terminates the trusteeship.

Only part of the UN process was completed, therefore, when the Trusteeship Council voted in favour of termination in May 1986. Britain, France and the USA voted for and the Soviet Union against. A final decision is still being awaited from the Security Council. The political future of Micronesia depends upon the precise mechanism by which the Security Council decides the trusteeship question. If a means of avoiding a substantive vote can be found, the USA will get what it wants. But if not, the Soviet Union is expected to exercise its veto to prevent the trusteeship from coming to an end. In that case the Americans would be stuck with their island territories and with the odium of being a colonial power in the Pacific.

For the sake of their image abroad the Americans want Micronesia to look as if it has been decolonised. But the appearance of decolonisation might be denied them.

6

Islands with a military future

Belau

Fly to Manila. Take the plane on to Guam, where the US Department of Defense spends $750 million a year. Then board an Air Micronesia flight to Yap in the western Carolines. You are on your way to an island group which has become famous for drafting the world's only nuclear free constitution. This is Belau, or, as it is just as commonly called, Palau. When I went I sat next to doll-like Japanese actresses who were going to Yap to film underwater sequences for a pornographic movie. Yap is also the place to buy high quality betel nut, which can then be traded in Belau. The red marks left by people who have spat in the dirt remind you that the people of the western Carolines are addicted to chewing betel.

Descending an hour later over the main Belauan island of Babeldaob you see little but jungle, and Airai airport terminal is nothing more than an elaborate shed, where you clear customs and take a bus to the capital, Koror. Here, as you walk for a kilometre past an untidy collection of buildings stained by rain and mould, you realise that this is among the smallest of would-be nations, a country of 15 000 people. Koror is smaller than many provincial towns in Papua New Guinea.

Belau is beautiful. The Rock Islands near Koror are one of the sights of the Pacific. Everywhere the vegetation is lush and the tropical waters are transparent. Viewed from the sea, the island of Babeldaob is a terrain of gentle green hills, with coral reefs offshore. The island was once headquarters of the Japanese colonial administration in Micronesia, and Koror was a sizeable Japanese town. But the Americans expelled the Japanese *en masse* in 1944, razing Koror to the ground.

Like the rest of the Trust Territory of the Pacific Islands, Belau will not be truly decolonised under the Compact of Free Association. Instead, the Belauans will be paid off, after a fashion, to make their small territory available for US military and strategic purposes. As part of the process of 'decolonisation' the island territories drew up constitutions in the late 1970s. Belau's constitution of 1979, to the alarm of US officials, included a unique nuclear free clause. Since then the USA has gone to extraordinary lengths to ensure that this clause is either overridden by popular vote or else bypassed so that American forces in the future will be free to bring nuclear weapons into the island state. Some Belauans support the Americans; others want to use the impasse over the nuclear free constitution as a way of getting more aid money from Washington; still others, led by Belauan activists such as Roman Bedor and Bernie Keldermans, simply want their land to be nuclear free. All the Islanders are in a bind. They have had plenty of food to eat and beer to drink under the Americans. Now they are in the position of depending on Uncle Sam for economic survival. But Uncle Sam has his price for helping Belau, a price which requires the Belauans not only to abandon their constitution but also to provide the US Department of Defense with options on 'defense sites' for possible use by the American military in the future.

'We drafted and approved a unique constitution that gave not only our people but the whole world an inspiration and hope from nuclear holocaust', says former Senator Moses Uludong, publisher of the pro-constitution newspaper *Rengel Belau*.[1]

According to article XIII, section 6, of the constitution, 'Harmful substances such as nuclear, chemical, gas or biological weapons intended for use in warfare, nuclear power plants, and waste materials therefrom, shall not be used, tested, stored or disposed of within the territorial jurisdiction of Palau without the express approval of not less than three-fourths (3/4) of the votes cast in a referendum submitted on this specific question.' The constitution also provides that any agreement authorising nuclear weapons in Belau is to be approved by at least 75 per cent of the votes in a referendum.

The making of the constitution in 1979 was not just a matter of high-level discussions in the Constitutional Convention. People held meetings in the villages to discuss their constitution and make suggestions. When the USA became aware that the constitution provided for a nuclear free zone, the US chief negotiator went to Belau and told the political leaders that America would not agree to free association until the nuclear free idea was dropped together with certain other provisions. A referendum on the nuclear free constitution went ahead on 9 July 1979. Ninety-two per cent of the voters approved it, but after a legal challenge in the Trust Territory High Court the new constitution was declared to be without legal standing.

At this point Belauan leaders produced a revised constitution designed to meet American objections and enable US military forces to bring nuclear weapons into Belau. A large majority voted to reject it. So the original, nuclear free version was again put to the people, who reaffirmed their original support for it in July 1980, and on this basis the islands gained a form of self-government in 1981. Since then the Islanders have been divided over the future of their country. Broadly speaking, younger political leaders with ties to the USA tend to favour the Compact of Free Association as the Americans want it, with nuclear and military strings attached; whereas older traditional leaders follow the anti-nuclear activists in defending the nuclear free constitution and opposing the military land options. The Belau government has mostly supported the American position.

A further plebiscite in the tortuous process of decolonising Belau came in February 1983. It was delayed by a month after the USA attempted to dictate the wording of the ballot so as to mislead voters into making a pro-nuclear decision. After a group of Belauans challenged the wording in a lawsuit, the ballot language was changed and voters once again opted to retain their nuclear free constitution. At the same time they voted in favour of free association with the USA. The question now was whether Belau had approved free association or not. The US State Department claimed that it had, and that the ballot on the nuclear issue was 'an internal referendum question'. It was up to Belau, Washington said, to bring its constitution into line with the Compact, in other words, to accept America's demand that the islands be kept open to the entry of nuclear weapons. The pro-constitution forces, led by traditional chief Ibedul Yutaka Gibbons, challenged this interpretation in a lawsuit and the Supreme Court of Belau upheld the challenge in August 1983. In the judgement of the Supreme Court, Belau had not approved free association because its terms were inconsistent with the constitution which the people supported: free association allowed nuclear weapons and substances into the islands; the constitution banned them.[2]

The Americans and their supporters among the islands' elite now made a concerted effort to get the people to accept a Compact which would serve America's military needs and force an amendment of the nuclear free constitution. A revised Compact emerged from talks between US Ambassador Fred M. Zeder II and Belauan Ambassador Lazarus E. Salii in May 1984. Four hundred pages long, written in English legalese, it was hardly a document which most Islanders would have understood even if they had been able to obtain a copy. Far from restricting America's military and nuclear freedom of action the revised Compact broadened it. Sweeping powers of intervention in Belau's affairs were guaranteed to the USA under clauses which would make the islands little more than a military colony if America so desired. The government of Belau was required to 'refrain from actions which the government of the United States determines, after consultation with that government, to be incompatible with its authority and responsibility for security and defense matters in or relating to Palau'. The USA could do whatever it thought necessary in exercising its 'full authority and responsibility for security and defense matters in or relating to Palau'.[3] Within 60 days Belau had to make available any land which the USA might need for military use in addition to the options on military sites already agreed upon.

In the limited time available before yet another plebiscite, pro-constitution groups attempted to alert people to the true nature of the revised Compact. KLTAL-RENG, an anti-nuclear organisation, some traditional chiefs, local politicians and the Catholic Women's Group held meetings in the villages and in the main town, Koror; they sent their best speakers to argue for the Constitution on the government radio station WSZB;

and shortly before the plebiscite on 4 September 1984, a co-alition of pro-constitution groups formed under the title of Osobel Belau (Save Palau Committee) and held a rally in Koror. The principal question which voters had to answer was confusing and unclear. A 75 per cent majority was required and despite a vigorous pro-Compact campaign by the Belau government, just over 66 per cent of the votes cast were in favour. The 1984 Compact of Free Association was therefore defeated, just as the earlier Compact lost in 1983.[4]

Yet another version of the Compact between the USA and Belau was put to the Islanders in February 1986. Once again, it represented a deal by which the USA will appear to decolonise Belau while in fact keeping the islands open to the American military for as long as the USA wishes. Under section 453(a), the defence and security arrangements remain in force for 50 years 'and thereafter until terminated or otherwise amended by mutual consent'. On the nuclear issue, the 1986 Compact was ingeniously worded so as to suggest that the USA intended not to 'use, store or dispose of nuclear ... weapons' in Belau, while at the same time guaranteeing that the USA would in fact be able to do these things. Under section 324, the USA 'has the right to operate nuclear capable or nuclear propelled vessels and aircraft within the jurisdiction of Palau without either confirming or denying the presence or absence of such weapons within the jurisdiction of Palau'. The Belau consti-tution specifically prohibits the use or storage of nuclear weapons or materials; yet to bring nuclear ships with nuclear missiles on board in and out of the waters of Belau is clearly to 'use' or 'store' them there. A 75 per cent vote was therefore also needed to ratify the 1986 Compact.[5]

The three-week political education campaign stressed the argument that the Compact was a good thing and would put money in people's pockets. Copies of the Compact in the Belauan language were available only a few days before the plebiscite, and many people remained confused about its effect on their nuclear free constitution. At 72.2 per cent in favour of the Compact, the final vote was higher than before, but still short of the 75 per cent needed to make the new political arrangement with the USA constitutional.

The Americans greeted the result enthusiastically,

Ambassador Fred Zeder describing his country as 'honored at this solid and unequivocal statement by the Belau people'.[6] In Belau itself President Lazarus Salii claimed that the vote confirmed his country's ratification of the Compact. But in July 1986 the Supreme Court of Belau ruled that the Compact of Free Association violated the clause of Belau's constitution which prohibits the use, testing, storage or disposal of nuclear weapons. The Judge commented that 'there was no way to get around the Constitution's intent, no matter how hard I searched'.[7] Two months later the appeals division of the Court confirmed the Judge's view that the Compact had not been ratified; and it went further, ruling that the plebiscite should have included a separate ballot question on the nuclear issue. So the Islanders were called to the polls again, in December 1986, once more failing to endorse the military and nuclear arrangements desired by both Washington and their own government. This time the vote fell to 66 per cent, 9 per cent short of the required figure.

The people of Belau have now voted seven times on the issue of their nuclear free constitution: three times in 1979 and 1980, when the USA was objecting to such a constitution as the basis for a form of self-government; and then again in 1983, 1984 and twice in 1986 in plebiscites on the Compact. The Supreme Court of Belau has ruled on three occasions that a nuclear Compact is inconsistent with the constitution unless it gets 75 per cent of the vote. The Americans have been mightily frustrated by the Belauans. And the US intention has been to hold out the carrot of Compact money long enough to make the Islanders yield. In a parody of democracy, the Americans have been making the Belauans vote again and again until they vote the 'right' way; and for Washington the 'right' way means the one which allows the USA nuclear access to the islands in the future.

The US argument is that, in taking on the job of defending Belau, US forces should be free to use whatever methods they think necessary. But no one seriously believes that America's primary motive for wanting military access to Belau is to protect the Islanders. Their small islands could be perfectly defended by a modest conventionally-armed force. What is at stake is rather US national security as defined in the Pentagon. In particular, the Americans want to have fallback positions for their military forces in case an anti-American regime gains power in the Philippines, and deprives them of military bases. The Filipino President Corazon Aquino, who replaced the corrupt Ferdinand Marcos in 1986, may yet be overwhelmed by a more thoroughgoing revolution in her country.

John C. Dorrance, a State Department Pacific specialist, has pointed out that one of the contingencies which would compel the US to put military bases in Belau would be 'loss of access to facilities in the Philippines. Under such circumstances the strategic importance of not only Palau, but also of Guam and the Northern Marianas, would increase as possible sites for the relocation of some US military operations presently at Subic Bay and Clark Air Base. ... In the event of war, the US might need to utilize contingency rights in Palau to provide protection of sea lanes running north-south between the Philippines and Palau ... '[8]

The Reagan Administration stated publicly in 1982 that: 'One of the prime reasons for the TTPI lease options is to provide the potential for at least a partial alternative in the event of restrictions on US use or access to allied facilities in the Western Pacific, including Clark and Subic in the Philippines.' Pointing out that the Compact in no way limited the movement of US warships and submarines through Micronesia, the Administration said that 'airfields and harbors located in Micronesia' would be considered for use as 'alternative or supplementary support areas for US naval forces' if this should prove necessary.[9] In other words the USA has not ruled out using Malakal Harbor in Belau as a submarine base. In any deal which is finally struck between the superpower and the micro-state, the USA is certain to be given options on Malakal Harbor, an ammunition storage dump, two airfields, one near Koror and the other on an island to the south called Angaur, together with a huge swathe of 12 000 hectares across the island of Babeldaob for use in training troops for jungle warfare. What it all amounts to is that the USA, if it wished, could virtually occupy the country. And the argument put by some Americans—that the USA 'might not even take up the

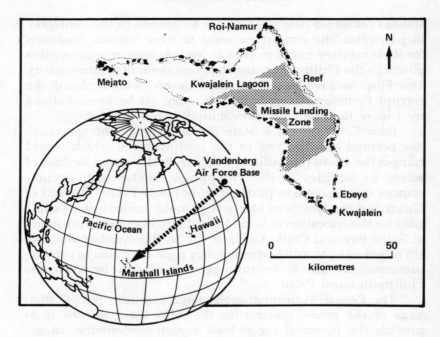

The US tests its intercontinental ballistic missiles by firing them from Vandenberg Air Force Base in California to Kwajalein Atoll in the Marshall Islands. Although the Marshall Islands have gained a form of semi-autonomy the Kwajalein Missile Range remains in American hands. Thousands of people displaced by the missile program live on the tiny island of Ebeye, across the water from the Army base at Kwajalein Island.

options'—is weak in the extreme. Why take so much trouble to negotiate the defence site options if there is no intention of using them?

Kwajalein Atoll

No part of the Pacific Trust Territory has been more affected by American strategic interests than Kwajalein, the world's largest atoll. With a land area of 17.6 square kilometres, the 93 islands and islets of Kwajalein enclose a huge lagoon of 2335 square kilometres in the Ralik or western chain of the Marshall Islands. Flying through Micronesia from the east the tourist is allowed out of the plane during the stopover at Majuro, the administrative centre of the Marshall Islands, but not at Kwajalein, where the air hostess announces that this is a military installation. Indeed it is, as the sign at the airstrip proclaims: 'Kwajalein Missile Range. Bucholz Army Air Field'. Sitting in the hot plane while a few people with security passes disembark, the visitor to Micronesia might be surprised to learn that Kwajalein is America's most important range for the testing of intercontinental ballistic missiles (ICBMs) and anti-ballistic missile systems. What happens here in the Pacific Islands, 7500 kilometres from the US mainland, is a vital contribution to the nuclear arms race, for it is into Kwajalein lagoon or nearby that missiles fired from Vandenberg Air Force Base in California splash down. A complex array of radar systems, missile tracking equipment, launch pads and test facilities has been built on the islands of Kwajalein atoll since the Americans first chose it as the target site for ICBMs in 1959. As Representative Robert J. Lagomarsino of California has said, Kwajalein now represents 'a tremendous capital investment in scientific instrumentation' and 'plays a key role in the development, testing and maintenance of America's long-range ballistic missile and anti-ballistic missile weapons systems'.[10]

In the relentless march of technological improvement in nuclear weapons both sides are striving to achieve pinpoint accuracy, so that a missile fired from the USA or the Soviet Union will land precisely on a missile-launching silo 10 000 kilometres away and thereby prevent enemy missiles from returning. Much of the testing done at Kwajalein is to make missiles more accurate, but the Army Ballistic Missile Defense Systems Command, which runs the facility, also experiments with methods of destroying incoming missiles by intercepting them. The US Army succeeded in shooting down a strategic missile near Kwajalein in June 1984, the first time such an interception had occurred, and in doing so gave encouragement to the military and industrial lobby favouring President Reagan's Star Wars initiative. The controversial MX missile, which represents a new generation of more deadly ICBMs in the American nuclear arsenal, has also been tested near Kwajalein. It is not surprising that the US government regards Kwajalein Missile Range as a vitally important national asset.

As elsewhere in the Marshall Islands the US military at Kwajalein moved people who happened to be in the way, beginning with the relocation of hundreds of Marshallese labourers from Kwajalein Island, which was a support base for nuclear testing, to Ebeye, an island of just 30 hectares lying five kilometres across the water to the north. People were moved to Ebeye in the early 1960s from Roi-Namur in Kwajalein atoll and nearby Lib Island. Then, when the Army assumed control of Kwajalein from the Navy in 1964, it proclaimed a 'Mid-Corridor' across the central two-thirds of the atoll as the impact area for incoming missiles. More people had to be moved to Ebeye from their home islands, which were now taken over by the military for use as tracking stations. So began the rapid urbanisation of the tiny island of Ebeye, which has become home not only to displaced Islanders but also to their relatives and to other Marshallese who perform menial work at the Kwajalein Island base, crossing each day by boat and being required to be off Kwajalein by sunset. Crowded on to Ebeye, in the densest concentration of population in the Pacific Islands, are about 8000 people, almost one in every four Marshallese.

The difference between Kwajalein Island, where the Americans live, and Ebeye, where the Marshallese live, was described by Representative John Seiberling in a Congressional hearing in 1984: 'In January 1982, I personally visited both Kwajalein Island and Ebeye island. The contrast couldn't be greater or more dramatic. Kwajalein is like Fort Lauderdale or one of our Miami resort areas, with palmtree-lined beaches, swimming pools, a golf course, people bicycling everywhere, a first-class hospital and a school; and Ebeye, on the other hand, is an island slum, overpopulated, treeless, filthy lagoon, littered beaches, a dilapidated hospital, and contaminated water supply, and so forth.'[11] The land used by the US Defense Department at Kwajalein is leased from the Marshallese landowners, about 5600 people. For years the landowners have protested over the military occupation of their islands, to some extent because they object to the missile program but mainly for economic reasons. They want more money, they have become used to the money economy and they have proved to be resourceful negotiators, skilled at putting pressure on a foreign government in Washington which always has plenty for the military but little for Ebeye.

The Kwajalein landowners' most dramatic and successful protest was *Operation Homecoming* in 1982, when about 1000 landowners reoccupied their islands, including some which lie in the path of approaching missiles. In the early stages of the protest, police arrested 15 people, and landowners marched past the gaol. As the sail-in continued and more camps were set up, *Operation Homecoming* became an opportunity for urbanised Islanders to rediscover an older way of life. 'Our people are happy living as they now are,' said the high-ranking chief Kotak Loeak, 'especially in the islands where there are no military facilities, nor armed guards to keep them in restricted areas. After years on crowded Ebeye Island, where we were forced to live by the US, we have discovered the joys of natural living, especially the freedom to move around, fish, plant and build living structures from the surrounding elements. I cannot begin to tell you how good the people feel . . . For the older people, the return brings tears of joy. For the children, it is an all new experience.'[12] One missile test, scheduled for 3 August 1982, was reportedly postponed when people who had camped on Roi-Namur refused to take cover.

The purpose of the reoccupation by the landowners was to force a change in the terms of the Compact of Free Association between the USA and the Marshall Islands, which at that stage gave the USA the Kwajalein Missile Range for 50 years. They also wanted better living conditions on Ebeye, higher lease moneys and more access to the islands of the atoll when missile tests were not in progress. But for months the USA refused to negotiate under pressure. In the words of Noel C. Koch, a Defense Department official: 'The Department of Defense desires a reasonable and fair relationship with the government and people of the Marshall Islands. However, we are not prepared to acquiesce in disruptive actions against the Kwajalein Missile Range, or to negotiate while they continue.'[13]

The Islanders regarded their 'disruptive actions' as peaceful resettlement of their own land. Many were women and children. Some had nuclear free Pacific posters. Some composed songs. And they were determined to stay. 'The old women remember where they grew up,' said Maria Lokjar, 'where they played, and where the wells were.'[14]

By October 1982, four months after *Operation Homecoming* began, the USA had no alternative but to negotiate. The result was a new three-year lease agreement with the landowners, the creation of a $10 million dollar capital works fund for Ebeye and a change in the long-term lease which would apply once the Marshalls entered into free association with the USA. That lease was now to run for 30 rather than 50 years.

When the Marshall Islanders finally voted on the Compact in September 1983, Kwajalein atoll, with 1411 ballots cast, voted 70.4 per cent against it, although the country as a whole voted by 58 per cent in favour.[15] The Kwajalein landowners, people displaced by US strategic interests, have nothing to gain from a fixed lease over a period of 15 years, with an American option on a further 15. Their best hope of extracting further concessions from the military at the missile range is a succession of short-term leases which can be renegotiated, and they have turned the endless delays in 'decolonising' Micronesia to their advantage. This was demonstrated when the 1982 lease expired in September 1985. The Islanders seized the opportunity to negotiate for more compensation. They refused an American request that the lease be extended for 60 days, did not accept $487 000 in rent for October and said they would not recognise the Compact of Free Association. The 1986 Compact provides more money—about $9 million a year in all—but the amount will stay the same for 15 years.

Repeating the tactics of 1982, small groups of landowners occupied three islands in the missile impact area, Meck, Enewetak and Omelek, while another group staged an occupation on the military base island of Kwajalein itself. The demonstrators on Kwajalein Island stayed for five months until US Army sentries evicted them by force in April 1986, dumping them on an island north of Ebeye. The Islanders walked back across the reefs to Ebeye and then adopted a new tactic. They formed a picket line on the wharf at Ebeye, preventing hundreds of workers from crossing each day to the military base and depriving the Army of its unskilled labour.

Many workers sympathised with the picketers. The picket broke up early in May 1986 after the US base commander ordered that sentries should 'shoot to wound' the Islanders.[16]

The situation of the Kwajalein landowners remains one of dependency created by the American missile range. It is far from one of hopelessness. Since the election of a municipal council in 1983 under Mayor Alvin Jacklick, and with more funds from the US government, things have improved on Ebeye. The sewerage system, while still inadequate, now works. The hospital has been renovated, and there are plans for an effective water supply. A causeway will eventually link Ebeye to other islands, relieving urban congestion. The people themselves have cleaned up the beaches and lagoon. Had the people not taken the initiative in 1982, little would have been done. The history of the US Army at Kwajalein suggests that it responds only to direct political pressure applied in Washington.

The future for the Marshallese at Kwajalein will be defined by the needs of the military. Once the Compact goes into effect their bargaining power will be weak. They will receive more money than they do now, though how much more is uncertain. In 1985 they got about $125 per person per quarter for funds distributed on a per capita basis, plus payments ranging from $1000 to $50 000 per quarter for chiefs, who then paid for education, health care and other expenses of numerous relatives. Whatever use the landowners make of this money, there is no doubt that the Kwajalein leader Ataji Balos was right when he told a US Congressional hearing in 1984 that the Kwajalein people are forced to 'live in a community in which the military intrusion on our lives not only dominates, but controls totally. Our future economic and social development will be within the parameters of what derives from military activity at Kwajalein.'[17]

7

'Where Aboriginals could not be'

When the Americans wanted atolls in the Pacific to let off their bombs, they moved the Islanders elsewhere, making token efforts to assist with resettlement. If the Americans did not recognise the Islanders' rights to their own homelands, they were at least aware of the Islanders' safety. In the case of the Aboriginal peoples of Australia, the attitude of the British and Australian authorities was more callous, because it derived from a deep indifference to whether people of another colour and cultural inheritance lived or died. Especially at the time of the test at Monte Bello in 1952, the British ignored the very existence of the Aborigines. Making use of sources such as the *Pocket Year Book of Western Australia* and the *Encyclopaedia Britannica*, the British estimated the population within 150 miles of the explosion as 715 people 'excluding full-blooded Aboriginals'.[1] Had they bothered to ask, the Western Australian government could have told them how many Aborigines lived in that part of the country. Statistics for the Gascoyne, Pilbara and Murchison regions in 1952 revealed an Aboriginal population of 4538. The Monte Bello bomb created fallout detected thousands of kilometres away at Rockhampton on the Queensland coast. But because of British secrecy and indifference, we will never know what it did to the people closest to Monte Bello. Of those people, the Aborigines would have been most at risk because of their preference for living with few clothes and in the open.

The extreme secrecy which hid this first British test from view was typical of the entire test program. Britain concealed the facts from Australia, and the Australian government obliged by controlling the press, using the system of 'D' notices to forbid newspaper coverage of matters supposedly vital to the national interest. Had Australians known more, the national interest would have been better protected. The British attitude was epitomised by the London official who warned of the dangers of saying too much to the Australians, who 'might disagree with the United Kingdom scientists' assessment of the risks or they might suggest that, in order to ensure that necessary precautions against contamination were in fact taken, Australians should be allowed closer to the scene of the test than we at present propose'.[2] Instead of facts, the British gave endless assurances that what they were doing was safe.

We do not know how much fallout the British atomic tests deposited over Australia. After the first mushroom cloud in 1952, men collected rainwater from roofs in a few places such as Rockhampton, Cairns and Brisbane on the east coast of Australia, 3600 kilometres away from the blast, and found radioactivity at 200 times normal background level in the Rockhampton water. But no one organised a comprehensive system of measuring fallout throughout Australia until the Menzies government finally set up an Atomic Weapons Tests Safety Committee three years later. The committee installed a network of 29 sampling stations using sticky paper and air filters to find out the levels of contamination in different parts of the country.

The system was seriously flawed in two ways. First, measuring fallout by waiting for it to adhere to sticky paper was ineffective, especially in determining the extent of contamination by radioactive rain. The rain did not stick to the paper. It washed away fallout already collected. And after it, the paper was no longer sticky. In the second place, the safety system favoured the British because the committee was not politically independent.

The whole purpose of the safety committee was to give Australia an independent voice in the test program. Menzies himself said that its members should not include anyone 'identified as having an interest in the success of defence atomic experiments'.[3] Despite this, the British authorities were given the right to vet the appointments to the committee. This allowed for one of their own people, Ernest Titterton, to be on the committee and to be its chairman from 1957. Titterton lived in Australia—he was Professor of Nuclear Physics at the Australian National University—but his political loyalties were to Britain and to the success of the British atomic weapons program. He had been in the British team which observed the Bikini tests in 1946 and had worked at Los Alamos. His confident assurances that the British atomic explosions were perfectly safe helped to smooth the way for the second series of tests at Emu Field in South Australia in 1953. Professor Mark Oliphant, a nuclear physicist who might well have protected Australian interests, was not appointed to the safety committee, because Titterton and the British thought he was a security risk.

Like Bikini and Enewetak atolls, the Great Victoria Desert of South Australia attracted the bomb testers. It seemed remote. Yet people lived in both the areas where atomic blasts were to take place, Emu Field and Maralinga. The homelands of the Ngalea people lie west of Maralinga; those of the Guguda include Maralinga; to the north live the Pitjantjatjara and the Yankunytjatjara; and to the west and south are lands occupied by the Mirning and Wirangu peoples. The Emu claypan is in Yankunytjatjara country.

Like other European occupiers of Australia since 1788, the atomic bomb men assumed that, because the land was not obviously full of people, it must be an empty and unused wasteland. In fact people were constantly moving through the desert in groups of up to 25 men, women and children or as families and individuals. They went to hunt and gather, to set up a temporary camp, to engage in ceremony or they were simply on their way to somewhere else. Before the atomic trials at Emu in 1953 an official visited the cattle stations of the area telling the white managers to warn the Aborigines about what was to happen, and a patrol officer made a check of Aboriginal movements. Yet as the official was to admit years later, it was impossible to protect Aborigines over such a vast region: 'They could be sitting behind a salt bush and you would never know: even low flying aircraft would not pick them up. So, in that sense, he would be a foolish man to guarantee that he could ensure us that there were no natives in the area . . .'[4]

Like the Pacific Islanders downwind of the *Bravo* explosion, Aborigines and some Europeans living north-east of Emu Field were dusted by radioactive fallout. Unlike the Pacific Islanders, however, the Aborigines were not believed when they said they were exposed. They described a black mist which rolled over the desert from the direction of the bomb and made people cough and vomit. Titterton, interviewed in 1980, said flatly that no such thing could 'possibly occur' and that to investigate it would be 'a complete waste of money and time'.[5] After careful consideration of the evidence from numerous witnesses, the Royal Commission into British Nuclear Tests in Australia concluded in 1985 that Titterton was wrong and that a black radioactive mist, generated by the bomb that exploded on 15 October 1953, had indeed enveloped people at Wallatinna, 173 kilometres north-east of Emu, and elsewhere.

Yami Lester, now blind, was a child of 10 or 11 when the black mist came. He heard the noise of an explosion. Later, he saw something coming from the south, 'black-like smoke. I was thinking it might be a dust storm, but it was quiet, just moving, as it looks like, through the trees and above that again, you know. It was just rolling and moving quietly.' Pingkayi, Lester's mother, remembers that she vomited from the effects of the mist, and others did as well. Lalli Lennon says that she and her two children vomited, suffered from diarrhoea and experienced fever and headache. Further downwind of the fallout cloud at Never Never, Mrs A. Lander saw an odd cloud that morning, the colour of a rain cloud but without 'the compact, rolling look that a rain cloud would have'. Instead, it was 'just a sort of a mass' depositing a fine, sticky dust.[6] The observations of these people, Aboriginal and non-Aboriginal, accord with the record of weather on the day the bomb went off. The main radioactive cloud 'preserved its identity to a remarkable extent and was clearly visible even after 24 hours', crossing the coastline near Townsville, over 2000 kilometres to the north-east, about 50 hours after the blast.[7] Aircraft which flew through the cloud at a distance of 1600 kilometres were found to be heavily contaminated with radioactivity. The black mist was probably a local pocket of concentrated fallout.

The Islanders of Rongelap and Utirik, covered with fallout from *Bravo* in 1954, have been regularly examined ever since. While the full effects of their exposure are still disputed, we know in clear outline what has happened to their health. All agree that they have suffered radiation injuries, and should be compensated for them. But in the case of the people who experienced the black mist, the very failure of the authorities to protect the population becomes an excuse for doing nothing. Without long-term studies of health like those conducted by the Brookhaven National Laboratory in the Marshall Islands, no one can say with final certainty that people were injured by the black mist. Yet obviously they were. If people's accounts of the mist itself have finally been believed, why should their insistence that it made them sick be brushed aside? Exposure to radiation at high levels causes lesions of the skin and vomiting, precisely the symptoms described by the Aborigines at Wallatinna. In 1985 the Nuclear Tests Royal Commission recommended that people exposed to the black mist should be listed on a national register of nuclear victims and be able to claim compensation from the Australian government. The government would then have to prove that each claimant was *not* injured.

When the British selected Maralinga in South Australia for their third atomic test site, they were delighted. The man in charge of the British tests, Sir William Penney, had been knighted for making the Monte Bello bomb go off in 1952 and for ushering his country into the select circle of atomic powers. Penney thought Maralinga was 'a first class site. It would give us all that we wanted for many years to come and I see no difficulty in testing 20 or more weapons here.' He was assured, wrongly, that 'this area is no longer used for aborigines'.[8] Maralinga lay within the Ooldea Aboriginal Reserve, which people frequently visited for ceremonial purposes and was important for its sacred sites and objects. To pave the way for the mushroom clouds, the South Australian government abolished the Ooldea Reserve in 1954 and a Native Patrol Officer, W. B. MacDougall, tried to remove the attractions of the Reserve area by taking away its sacred objects. Neither of these measures stopped the traditional owners of the Maralinga site and other Aborigines from continuing to traverse the area.

MacDougall knew that Aboriginal people were walking

through Maralinga country, and that a comprehensive survey of their movements was vital. 'It is important,' he wrote in 1954,'that any nomadic occupation of prohibited areas should be well known to me, so that any measures considered necessary for the safety and well-being of the aboriginal people can be taken with confidence.'[9] But over the next three years, and especially while the bombs were exploding over Maralinga in 1956 and 1957, MacDougall was a frustrated man, deliberately ignored by officials. A colleague described him as 'a good bushman [who] related well to the Pitjantjatjara people and picked up some of their language. He felt his role was to articulate the interests of these people. ... He felt unable to convince the Woomera hierarchy that these people had a point of view. I felt that with the resources we were given, we had a hopeless task to guarantee that all Aborigines were kept out of the prohibited area. I am sure that was MacDougall's view. He saw himself pretty much as a lone figure.'[10] MacDougall annoyed his superiors for what was called his 'lamentable lack of balance' and for 'placing the affairs of a handful of natives above those of the British Commonwealth of Nations'.[11]

MacDougall's proposed survey never took place, and when the British let off their bombs in 1956 and 1957 Aborigines were within the Prohibited Zone. The Safety Committee lied to the Menzies government. It claimed that 'strict continuous ground and air patrols' would ensure that no Aborigines were within the zone. Nothing like this occurred. About four days before the atomic explosion of 27 September 1956, 24 Aborigines were seen half-way between Maralinga and Lake Maurice. One day before the test, a newly-appointed and inexperienced patrol officer reported frankly from the Giles Meteorological Station:'Unable to satisfy myself no natives south of mentioned line. Have not been there. Unable to penetrate without own vehicle and radio. Hear none Mt Harriot area'.[12] Despite this disturbing admission, the bomb was exploded as planned. The peak local fallout from this bomb will never be known because it fell in the area between two sticky paper stations. Fallout contaminated the east coast of Australia, more than 2000 kilometres away, in a wide band which stretched from Coffs Harbour in New South Wales 1500 kilometres north to Townsville in Queensland.

To report sightings of Aborigines was not the way to

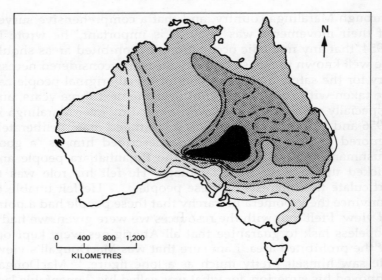

Distribution of radioactive fallout over Australia from the Buffalo 4 test at Maralinga, 22 October 1956, as measured by sticky paper collectors. The heavier the shading the more concentrated the fallout. The four Maralinga tests of 1956 produced 'a large increase' in radioactive iodine—131 in the thyroids of sheep and cattle in central and eastern Australia. (Source: The Report of the Royal Commission into British Nuclear Tests in Australia, *pp.298—9)*

please the authorities in charge of atomic explosions. When a member of the Australian Radiation Detection Unit stationed at Mt Wooltarlinna said he had seen hunting fires which were probably in the Prohibited Zone, he was asked if he realised 'what sort of damage' he would be doing 'by finding Aboriginals where Aboriginals could not be'.[13] The damage to be avoided, of course, was to the British test program, not to the people being injured by it.

Air patrols in search of Aborigines were little more than token gestures for the sake of favourable publicity. The British bothered to search the Maralinga zone from the air only twice during the 1956 tests, and the man in charge of the search program in 1957 says it was 'like looking for a needle in a haystack given the vastness of the area and the means at our disposal'. Since 'the country was too vast to cover on a grid basis', the reality of air searches was that the plane 'really just flew up the road and not over the country'.[14] To have been seen, Aborigines would have had to be on the road or close by, rather than following traditional routes determined by the presence of water and food. Royal Air Force crews, ignorant of Aboriginal ways of life and told simply to look out for smoke by day and fire by night, were in any case travelling 150 metres above the ground at speeds of 400 or 500 kilometres an hour. The chances of finding individual Aborigines on the desert below were almost nil.

On patrol in 1960 officers encountered 14 Aborigines just north of Nurrari Lakes. They had been living permanently in the area, and said they heard the atomic bombs at Maralinga a few years before. The discovery proved what MacDougall had known all along:'natives have been living well inside the Maralinga Prohibited Zone continuously from before the establishment of the Atomic Weapons Testing Grounds.'[15] Henry Anderson, one of a number of Aborigines living in the Maralinga zone during the British tests, remembers seeing a bomb go off soon after a plane flew over. He probably saw the air-burst explosion of 11 October 1956. He said the 'smoke' had 'killed or hurt' sacred sites at Lake Dey Dey and Bulgunya, and that 'white people thought there was nothing sacred in that place and therefore they let the bombs go or threw the bombs over there'.[16] Other Aboriginal people recall hearing the atomic explosions, feeling the ground shake and watching the mushroom clouds. Afraid, people put out camp fires and hid from aircraft.

One Aboriginal family set out in mid-1956 on a trip from the Everard Ranges to Ooldea, following the traditional rock hole route and unaware that the Ooldea Aboriginal settlement had been closed to make way for the atomic bombs. In May 1957, walking through Maralinga, they were found by a group of engineers at the site where the British had exploded a 1.5 kiloton bomb the year before. One of the Army men later remembered the incident:'The warning signs were no good to the Aborigines, they couldn't understand them. They came to us with a billy for water, and we ran a geiger counter over them. The readings were pretty frightening '[17] The four Aborigines were given showers in the health physics caravan to remove radioactive contamination and then taken by vehicle to Yalata, away from the Maralinga range. Nothing more was done for them. For the Range Commander, all that mattered was to keep the scandal hushed up. He told the Nuclear Tests Royal Commission:'This would be a rather sensitive matter and we were all very guarded in anything that we had to say so that preferably it didn't get out from the range. I made this known to the men on the range that references to the incident were not to take place at all, particularly as they were under the Defence Special Undertakings Act ... '[18] In Canberra the UK High Commission reassured London that everything poss- ible was being done to keep news of the incident from the press. The cover-up worked, and it was not until 1980 that the Australian government admitted the truth.

Even with the truth established, however, the British Commander of the Maralinga Range would not admit to making serious mistakes:

> Q   ...the fact that security had been breached, so that this family had got right into the contaminated area, did you suggest to your superiors that something further should be done to provide adequate security on the range?
> A   The system itself was clearly sound. I know it had one or two breaches.
> Q   But it was pretty obvious by this stage, was it not, that it could not have been operating to secure the most sensitive of areas?
> A   This is so.[19]

Detail by detail, the accumulated evidence points to one conclusion: the British atomic bomb men, supported by Australian scientists, proceeded with the Maralinga explosions knowing that people were in the Prohibited Zone and were therefore likely to be injured or killed. The few like MacDougall who criticised the authorities for their disregard of Aboriginal safety were ignored or told to keep quiet. The patrols on the ground and in the air, as those who undertook them knew, were unsystematic and did not succeed in keeping Aboriginal people away from the testing range. Yet through- out the tests the Australian and British governments claimed to have provided comprehensive protection for the desert peoples. The claims were lies, fed to the Australian public to allay mounting criticism of the entire test program.

After the British tests officially ended in 1957, they continued secretly until 1963 in what was called the Maralinga Experimental Programme, a fact which the British Ministry of Defence did not admit until the 1980s. While this did not involve large atomic blasts, it caused the dispersal of radioactive materials such as beryllium, uranium−238 and plutonium. The British, obsessive about secrecy, excluded Australians from the firing sites at all these minor trials, and even today they remain tight-lipped about exactly what happened. But we do know that radioactive materials were burnt in fires and spread over the desert by conventional high explosives in experiments which were supposed to simulate nuclear accidents such as bomber crashes. The explosions, far more numerous than the atomic bomb tests themselves, contaminated concrete, cables, rocks and soil and have poisoned parts of the desert. They left behind some of the most serious radiological hazards at the test sites. During the Nuclear Tests Royal Commission it was suggested to one of the prominent British scientists that 'the planning foundation for your work was that radioactive contamination of Australia may be politically acceptable but not for the UK'.[20] He agreed.

The British have not yet cleaned up the Maralinga and Emu test sites, though they made a couple of inadequate attempts to do so in the 1960s. During *Operation Brumby* in 1967 they covered land around each major test site with top soil, removed metal debris and, using a grader, attempted to reduce the hazard from plutonium by mixing it with soil. They also tried to make the test range blend into the landscape by taking down fences and warning signs, in the hope that people would not find it. *Operation Brumby* made the future clean-up of the sites more difficult. Examining them in 1984 and 1985, the Australian Radiation Laboratory estimated that there are between 25 000 and 50 000 fragments contaminated with plutonium in the Taranaki area of Maralinga; they are small pieces of steel or alloy coated on one side with plutonium, one of the most dangerous substances known. Now that they are mixed in with soil, they are far less recoverable. Once again, the touching faith of the Australian Safety

Committee in British promises has proved unfounded. The Committee expressed only minor reservations when it assured the Australian Prime Minister in 1967 that Maralinga and Emu had been made radiologically safe.

The folly of making radioactive dumps look like the surrounding countryside was shown by the salvage operations at Maralinga in the mid-1970s. Aborigines from the Yalata Mission were given permission to dismantle and take away disused buildings and equipment on the test range and they took the opportunity of digging up lathes, trailers, Land Rovers and hydraulic jacks from the pits where the British had buried them. They also walked freely through the area and camped out. Suddenly in May 1976 they were told to stop digging and put what they had excavated back into the pits. The Chief Defence Scientist of the Department of Defence warned against any further excavations at Maralinga, in view of the investigations being made about radioactive hazards. After three years of bureaucratic delays, the Australian government finally decided in 1979 that it had never intended people to dig up buried equipment. By then, the salvage was almost finished.

Under a South Australian land rights act of 1984, 76 420 square kilometres of land surrounding the British test sites went back to the Aboriginal traditional owners, and the South Australian government intends to return all the land eventually. Many people are keen to return to their country, and a group of about 80 has been living in the Lake Dey Dey region since 1982. They hunt kangaroo, and much of their food is traditional rather than European. The Maralinga sacred sites and ceremonial grounds have not been forgotten, and a number of Aborigines wish to live in much closer association with them. But they fear the poison which the British spread over the land. Perhaps more than anyone, the Aboriginal traditional owners want Emu and Maralinga to be properly cleaned up. Their fears are justified. Not only are there thousands of small bits of radioactive metal in the soil at Maralinga, but little is known about the levels of plutonium in the animals and plants of the area. At one site rabbits have dug burrows around the edges of the concrete caps which cover pits containing 20 kilograms of plutonium. Someone with bare feet could receive a fatal dose of plutonium simply from a tiny piece of metal in the soil; and as happened at Bikini, the food chain could become dangerously radioactive. Even breathing dust-laden air might be a hazard.

Whereas the Americans kept a close watch on the Bikinians who went back to their homeland in the 1970s, the Australian authorities are only now beginning to accept that a problem exists. The first Australian study of the effects of radiation on Aboriginal people did not appear until 1981, and two others have followed. But they are inconclusive. We know that a number of Pitjantjatjara people have died from thyroid cancers and leukaemias which could be the result of exposure to radiation, but the statistics of births, deaths, health care and illness are too poor to establish a causal link. Once again, the very indifference of white society in Australia to the original occupiers of the land stands in the way of the most elementary justice. As for the British, they continue to contest even the need for a clean-up of the test sites. The Nuclear Tests Royal Commission recommended an immediate clean-up, so thorough that Emu and Maralinga would be 'fit for unrestricted habitation by the traditional Aboriginal owners as soon as practicable',[21] and that Britain should pay, as it should also pay for the restoration of the Monte Bello Islands to a safe state. But reports from London suggest that the British government has no intention of footing the bill for removing Britain's radioactive legacy on the other side of the world. After talks in 1986 the British and Australian governments agreed to investigate the methods and costs of a clean-up of nuclear debris, but the British Foreign Secretary Sir Geoffrey Howe did not say Britain would pay for it. 'UK ducks Maralinga clean-up', said the headline in the *Sydney Morning Herald*.[22] The newspaper was proved right later in the year, when the British said they would share with Australia the cost of preliminary studies into a clean-up. Over the next two years anthropologists, biochemists and other experts were to measure contamination at Emu and Maralinga, and assess the risks it poses to people living, breathing, and eating there. But the crucial point was that Britain had still not admitted legal or moral responsibility for the radioactive problem which its bombs created.

The long-term consequences of the British H—bomb tests at Christmas Island remain a mystery. Unlike the USA, Britain has never released information about the doses of radiation received by task force men during the Pacific tests. Some British ex-servicemen recall that not all went well. The H—bomb of 28 April 1958 is said to have sparked 'a line of thunderstorms' according to a pilot whose Shackleton bomber had to be decontaminated after flying through the storms; and a meteorologist says radioactive rain fell on Christmas Island after the same blast.[23]

Oddly, most of the 300 or so Gilbertese plantation workers on Christmas were evacuated during the Malden Island tests but not for those which took place close to Christmas itself. Instead, the Islanders went to offshore vessels so as to be under cover when the flash occurred. The same thing happened during the 1962 American tests, though as the US series continued more and more people stayed on shore. There they 'waited with bowed heads and closed eyes for the countdown, for "flash" was still the danger. They were then free to go outside and see for the first time the boiling flames of the "mushroom" cloud and experience the delayed shock waves and the roar of the explosion.'[24] From the scraps of information available, the British appear to have been as careless in the Pacific as in Australia.

8

Raison d'état

The *Rainbow Warrior*, the 40-metre flagship of the international Greenpeace organisation, sailed into Waitemata Harbour, Auckland, on Sunday 7 July 1985. It tied up at Marsden wharf. The first of its Pacific missions was over, the people of Rongelap having been ferried to their new home elsewhere in the Marshall Islands in May. Its second mission, a protest cruise to the French nuclear testing site at Moruroa in French Polynesia, was still to come. The plan was to take a number of well-known Tahitian independence activists on the voyage together with doctors who could carry out independent medical examinations in the French territory.[1]

Members of Greenpeace in New Zealand were not the only people who had followed the movements of the *Rainbow Warrior* with interest and anticipation. Sometime earlier in the year the French nuclear testing agency DIRCEN (Direction des Centres d'essais Nucléaires) under Admiral Henri Fages expressed concern about the new Greenpeace campaign, claiming that Greenpeace intended to use light canoes to land people on Moruroa during the 1985 tests. Officials at the highest levels of the French government, impressed by the argument, authorised the expenditure of perhaps $600 000 to fund a secret operation against the *Rainbow Warrior*: they were President François Mitterrand's personal chief-of-staff General Jean-Michel Saulnier, together with General Jeannou Lacaze, chief-of-staff of the armed forces, and the Defence Minister Charles Hernu, nicknamed Hernucléaire for his enthusiastic endorsement of France's independent nuclear force.

Their orders went to Admiral Pierre Lacoste, head of

83

France's foreign spying agency, the DGSE (Direction Générale de la Sécurité Extérieure) and from him to the man in charge of the DGSE's Action Division, Colonel Jean-Claude Lesquer. Greenpeace's threat to French security was so seriously regarded that the list of Frenchmen plotting against Greenpeace began to resemble a Who's Who of France's top military and intelligence staff.

Those who carried out the orders came from the demi-monde of zealous patriots, thugs and right-wing extremists working for the DGSE. The first to reach New Zealand was Christine Cabon, 33, travelling under the assumed name Frédérique Bonlieu, who infiltrated Greenpeace during May and took numerous photographs of harbours and beaches in the North Island. Posing as a geomorphologist and archaeologist, she worked for Greenpeace by producing anti-nuclear pamphlets in French. When she left New Zealand after about three weeks she had detailed inside knowledge of the organisation. From there she went to French Polynesia, supposedly to attend a conference being held in Tahiti on coral reefs, but in fact it was to gather information about opponents of nuclear testing such as the well-known anthropologist Bengt Danielsson and his wife Marie-Thérèse. Since the Danielssons have never made a secret of their beliefs, she probably discovered nothing that has not already been published in their monthly column in *Pacific Islands Monthly*.

Meanwhile French agents in New Caledonia arranged to charter a yacht to take them to New Zealand. Late in May a man calling himself Raymond Velche walked into Noumea Yacht Charters and paid two million Pacific French francs or about $15 000 to hire the 11.6 metre *Ouvéa* for seven weeks. A fortnight later, on 13 June, the *Ouvéa* left Noumea for Norfolk Island and New Zealand. On board were Dr Xavier Maniguet, possibly a spy, and three others, all DGSE agents from the underwater training school in Corsica: 'Velche' (Roland Verge, an agent for 11 years and an experienced frogman), 'Eric Audrenc' (Gerald Andries) and 'Jean-Michel Berthelo', whose real name, somewhat disappointingly, is Jean-Michel Bartelo. After visiting a number of towns along the coast, they anchored at Whangarei, a small centre about one and a half hours' drive from Auckland. There they established a base camp for the

Above *Radar and monitoring facilities on the Kwajalein Atoll island of Roi-Namur. The radar dish on the right is part of the US Air Force's Pacific Barrier anti-satellite detection system, linking with stations in the Philippines and Guam. It tracks Soviet satellites over the Pacific. (Photo courtesy of Greenpeace)* Below **Baker,** *the second US atomic bomb test at Bikini Atoll, 25 July 1946. The explosion lifted the 26 000-ton battleship* **Arkansas** *on one end. (Photo: US Navy)*

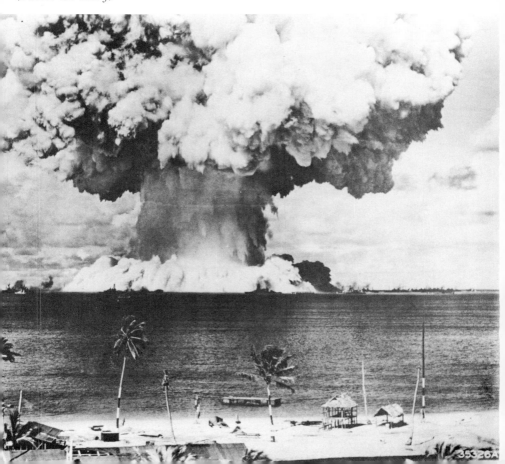

Above *The mushroom cloud from one of the earliest American thermo-nuclear explosions in the Marshall Islands, 1952. (Photo: US Atomic Energy Commission, from 'Half Life')*
Left *Lewis Strauss, Chairman of the US Atomic Energy Commission, at a White House press conference, March 1954. He announced that the people of Rongelap and Utirik atolls in the Marshall Islands had been accidentally exposed to radioactive fallout. (Photo: Universal Newsreel, from 'Half Life')*

Above *Thousands of tonnes of radioactive soil and scrap metal lie under this huge concrete dome on Runit Island, Enewetak Atoll, Marshall Islands. The radioactive debris was bulldozed there under the American clean-up program from 1977 to 1980. The dark patch in the lagoon to the left is a crater created by a bomb explosion in the 1950s. (Photo: Kousei Shimada)*
Below *Men clamber across the face of the concrete dome on Runit Island, soon after construction finished in 1980. Covering thousands of tonnes of radioactive debris from US nuclear tests, the site is off-limits to human beings for the next 24 000 years. (Photo: US Government)*

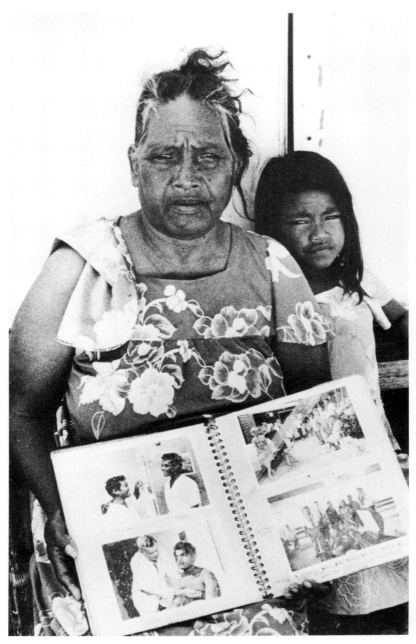

Mijjua Anjain of Rongelap Atoll shows photographs of her son Lekoj, who was a baby at the time of the Bravo nuclear test. Lekoj Anjain died from leukemia at the age of nineteen, a death which US experts admitted 'may have been related to radiation exposure'. (Photo: Dennis O'Rourke, from 'Half Life')

Above *Tanira Jorju of Rongelap Atoll holds her grandson, Kimo, born to parents who were children at the time of the* Bravo *fallout in 1954. She blames Kimo's retardation on the bomb. (Photo: Dennis O'Rourke, from 'Half Life')*

Below *Evacuees from Rongelap Atoll, brought by the Greenpeace vessel* Rainbow Warrior, *are welcomed at their new home of Mejato Island, May 1985. (Photo courtesy of Greenpeace)*

Above *Ellen Boas of Rongelap Atoll with her grandson, pointing to the scar left after her operation in America to remove thyroid tumours caused by exposure to fallout from* Bravo *in 1954. (Photo: Gary Kildea, from 'Half Life')*
Below *The lagoon side of the beach at Ebeye Island, Kwajalein Atoll. More than 8000 people live here, in the densest concentration of population in the Pacific Islands. About 5600 of them are Kwajalein landowners, displaced from other islands of the atoll by the American testing program. (Photo: Giff Johnson)*

Above *Greenpeace crew on board the* Rainbow Warrior, *Marshall Islands, May 1985. After moving the people of Rongelap Atoll to a new home on Mejato, the* Rainbow Warrior *sailed via Vanuatu to New Zealand, where it was bombed by French secret service agents. (Photo courtesy of Greenpeace)*
Below *David Lange, Prime Minister of New Zealand, takes a seat beside George Schultz, American Secretary of State in a meeting at Manila, June 1986, where Schultz later announced that the US had withdrawn its security guarantee to New Zealand because the Lange government had banned visits by nuclear ships. (Photo: AAP)*

Greenpeace commemorates the death of Fernando Pereira on board the Rainbow Warrior, *one year after it was bombed in Auckland harbour by the French secret service. Paris, 10 July 1986. (Photo courtesy of Greenpeace)*

operation against the *Rainbow Warrior*, bought some gear and hired two cars. New Zealand is a country where people tend to know other people's business, especially in small country towns. Without being aware of it, just by being French the DGSE agents stood out like sore thumbs. People later remembered almost everything they did while in Whangarei.

The frogmen from the *Ouvéa* then met up with two spies whose subsequent arrest by New Zealand police was to be the catalyst of the whole affair. They went by the names of 'Sophie-Clair and Alain Turenge' and their passports gave their citizenship as Swiss. Supposedly a married couple travelling innocently around the north island of New Zealand—she a school teacher and he a company manager—they were in fact Captain Dominique Prieur and Major Alain Mafart, both French secret service agents employed by the DGSE. During the weekend of the *Rainbow Warrior's* arrival, they travelled in a hired campervan to rendezvous with the frogmen about 200 kilometres north of Auckland. Plans for the attack were discussed and equipment moved from the *Ouvéa* to the campervan.

Yacht and campervan then moved south along the coast. About 80 kilometres north of Auckland, two men came ashore from the *Ouvéa* in a French-made Zodiac rubber dinghy. With explosives and diving equipment, they were taken in the campervan to Auckland Harbour. About 8 pm on the night of 10 July, they took a dinghy across the harbour towards Marsden Wharf, dived beneath the *Rainbow Warrior* and fixed explosives on the starboard side and on the propeller. One diver was seen by members of a boating club coming ashore at Okahu Bay about 9.30 pm. Behind them they had left a trail of tell-tale evidence, including an airtank, an outboard motor and an inflatable boat.

While the men were taken north by the campervan to make their escape in the *Ouvéa*, crew members of *Rainbow Warrior* were discussing the problems they could expect on the voyage into the French test zone. The meeting finished about 11 pm. Some people went ashore, some to bed, others to a birthday party in the galley. Peter Willcox, the captain, was jolted awake by an explosion about 11.45 pm. 'I got to the engine room door about 20 seconds after the first explosion, and the water was just three feet below deck level. I was shocked. It just didn't make sense.' Water was pouring into the engine room through a hole two metres wide. First mate Martin Gotje thought something in the engine room had blown. Then came a second explosion, about two minutes after the first. More water gushed into the old North Sea trawler, which quickly keeled over into the half-submerged position which press photographers were to record for the world's media the following morning and which was soon to become a symbol of state-sponsored terrorism by France. The Greenpeace photographer, Fernando Pereira, was drowned when he went to rescue his cameras. His body was recovered by New Zealand Navy divers the day after the attack.

The message which Greenpeace International cabled to its sister offices in Europe, North America and Australia told the story:

> URGENT URGENT URGENT. APPROXIMATELY TWO HOURS AGO, RAINBOW WARRIOR SUNK BY TWO EX-PLOSIONS IN AUCKLAND HARBOR, NEW ZEALAND. SABOTAGE SUSPECTED. VERY LITTLE NEWS FORTH-COMING AT PRESENT. ONE CREW MEMBER MISSING. PLEASE DO NOT, REPEAT NOT, CALL AUCKLAND OF-FICE, AS TELEPHONES ARE JAMMED. WILL HAVE MORE INFO IN HOUR OR SO.

When the chairman of Greenpeace USA, Peter Bahouth, arrived in Auckland on 11 July he was greeted with the news of the sinking of the *Rainbow Warrior*: 'I went to the harbor immediately. When I got there, the *Rainbow Warrior*'s crew was standing around on the dock at Marsden Wharf. They were half-naked and cold. It was raining, and no one was saying anything. They were all just staring at what you could still see of the boat.'

Charles Montan, political counsellor at the French embassy in Wellington, quickly discounted the possibility of France's involvement in the sinking. 'The French government does not deal with its opponents in such ways,' he said. But numerous witnesses were soon volunteering information to the special investigation squad set up by Detective Superintendent Allan Galbraith. The air tanks, the dinghy, the *Ouvéa* itself, the campervan, the odd French people who had suddenly come and gone from the small towns north of Auckland: all had been noticed and were reported to police, who rapidly reconstructed events leading to the bombing. Forestry workers who had spoken to the French when they rendezvoused in a forest in Northland wrote down registration numbers in the dirt. The boating club members who saw one of the frogmen come ashore noted particulars of the van he got into, and immediately alerted the police. Someone in Whangarei remembered the French drawing stick figures of frogmen while having a meal at a restaurant.

Warned by police to be on the alert for the return of the hired campervan, Newmans Motor Caravans of Auckland quietly gave the tip-off which led to the arrest of the 'Turenges', Prieur and Mafart. Charged first with passport irregularities, the couple soon faced more serious charges of arson and murder. A few days later, on 26 July, warrants for the arrest of the frogmen of the *Ouvéa* were issued in New Zealand. The police were right in their suspicions but they were too late to catch the three French underwater experts. The *Ouvéa* had sailed straight for Norfolk Island after the bombing and disappeared somewhere between there and New Caledonia. It never returned to Noumea. The frogmen turned up in Paris towards the end of August, only to disappear again. One theory which seemed less fantastic the longer the affair continued was that the frogmen, having scuttled their yacht at sea, were picked up by the French nuclear submarine *Rubis*, transported from there to Moruroa and flown home to France.

By the first week of August two French weeklies, *L'Evènement du Jeudi* and *VSD*, were claiming that the 'Turenges' had links with French security. The press in France has a habit of keeping silent for the sake of *raison d'état*. This time, however, the newspapers were playing an investigative role. Their journalists obviously had good sources in the DGSE; and they began asking whether the DGSE might have been involved in the bombing. President Mitterrand, already under siege from the Right, was quick to sense the political danger in a cover-up. Assuring the Prime Minister of New Zealand that he abhorred 'the criminal attack on your territory which no excuse can justify', Mitterrand ordered a top-level inquiry.

As special commissioner he chose the respected Gaullist Bernard Tricot, a man whom the Right could not accuse of special pleading in favour of the Socialist government. Nothing if not intelligent, Tricot duly produced a report which admitted what could no longer be denied, but he exonerated the French secret service on the main charge of having bombed the *Rainbow Warrior*. At the same time, in masterly fashion, Tricot preserved his own reputation by emphasising that he did not know everything and might have been lied to.

In the Tricot report France officially admitted that the Defence Minister Charles Hernu had authorised a French intelligence operation 'to forecast and anticipate Greenpeace actions'. Christine Cabon was indeed a French agent sent to infiltrate Greenpeace in New Zealand. The task of the 'Turenges', also agents of the DGSE, was to provide information about the *Rainbow Warrior* and identify her crew. The three DGSE frogmen were supposed to be 'practising sailing in the South Pacific zone' and investigating the possibility of becoming crew members on a Greenpeace voyage in the future. Tricot did not think any of these people planted mines on the hull of the *Rainbow Warrior*.

The obvious question left unanswered by Tricot was why France would bother to send a team of highly trained divers merely to collect information. As one French politician commented: 'The Tricot report takes the French people for imbeciles. It would have us believe that one sends frogmen only to take photographs when it is clear to everyone that France gave itself over to an act of terrorism.' The report was greeted with derision everywhere. Cartoonists had a field day. The Prime Minister of New Zealand, David Lange, said it was so transparent that it could not even be a whitewash: 'The fact is that we've had operatives of French government intelligence agencies in New Zealand for some time. The French government is, of course, involved. New Zealand needs to have evidence of some contrition on the part of France because of that direct challenge to our sovereignty. Friendship is strained when you have a nation that is constantly pounding the ocean atolls with nuclear testing and has spies in our country.' Tricot himself probably did not expect to be believed. Within a few days he was speculating that the three frogmen might have bombed the *Rainbow Warrior* after all.

The release of the Tricot report did not produce public outrage in France. Almost no one thought the government should apologise to New Zealand, nor were there demands that the secret service be curbed. On the contrary, the principal complaint of the French public was that the *Rainbow Warrior* operation had been bungled. President Mitterrand grabbed the opportunity to reassert national pride in France's nuclear force and its intelligence services. In a quick trip across the world designed as a symbol of French national sovereignty, Mitterrand visited Moruroa in September 1985, stopping only in French Guiana to witness the launching of a rocket. On Moruroa Mitterrand was defiant of South Pacific opinion. Any foreign government challenging the French presence in this part of the world, he said, was an 'adversary'. In Paris, on his return, he told journalists that no one who had worked at Moruroa from the beginning had suffered from the effects of radioactivity; France would make sovereign decisions on everything touching its national interests; it would continue to test nuclear bombs; and the South Pacific governments were invited to send their Prime Ministers to Moruroa. The French, from left to right, liked what Mitterrand said. Communist Party leader Georges Marchais described the tests as vital to France as a nuclear power, while Jacques Toubon, leader of the Gaullist Rassemblement pour la République, said the trip had been a necessary affirmation of France's place in the Pacific. The Prime Ministers of New Zealand and Australia were rather less impressed. David Lange called Mitterrand's visit to Moruroa 'an obscene gesture'. Bob Hawke not only refused the invitation to go to the French test site, but had 'one message and one message alone' for the French President: 'If President Mitterrand is so interested to prove to everyone in our region just how absolutely safe these tests are, there is one logical conclusion that follows. Take his tests back to France and have those absolutely safe tests in metropolitan France.'

Mitterrand's patriotic dash to Moruroa was not enough to stop more of the truth about the *Rainbow Warrior* emerging within a few days. In a detailed, informed account of the chain of command involved in the Greenpeace plot, the Paris daily newspaper *Le Monde* cut the ground from beneath the Tricot version of events, showing that the Greenpeace plot had been authorised and funded at high levels within the French government. Faced with these revelations, the government was compelled to admit what it had been denying for the previous two months: the sinking of the environmentalists' ship had been done on orders after all. Lies had been told since 10 July. Exactly as most people in the South Pacific thought, France had sent its secret agents on a mission of violence to stop the Greenpeace campaign against French testing. Protesting that he had been deceived by his officials in the Defence Ministry, the Minister Charles Hernu resigned. Admiral Pierre Lacoste was sacked as head of the DGSE after refusing to answer questions about the affair put to him by the government. In the tradition of secret service chiefs who see themselves as above the mere government of the day, Lacoste said he would be placing the lives of brave French agents in peril if he told the politicians all he knew.

The bombing of the *Rainbow Warrior* achieved the opposite of what France intended. Instead of putting an end to Greenpeace's 1985 campaign in French Polynesia, it invigorated that campaign far beyond the dreams of the organisers. Contributions from sympathisers poured into Greenpeace offices. Throughout most of August and September the attention of the international media focussed on French testing at Moruroa to an unprecedented degree. As the *Greenpeace*, the new flagship of the ecology group, reached French Polynesia in early October, it was guaranteed worldwide publicity. Time bought on satellites and a sophisticated television transmission system enabled *Greenpeace* to relay live coverage of its voyage to the nuclear atolls of the Tuamotu Archipelago. The French responded by placing a 2000-tonne frigate at the disposal of journalists.

Four other protest vessels, *Alliance, Breeze, Varangian* and *Vega* sailed from New Zealand to French Polynesia in what was called the Pacific Peace Flotilla. *Greenpeace* broke down, *Breeze* turned back and *Vega* was boarded and seized by the French after it sailed inside the 12-mile territorial limit, while trying to stop a nuclear test at Moruroa. The French Navy held the crew of *Vega* in detention for a week, and they were later deported. By early November the crew of *Varangian* alone was keeping watch on the 1985 test series. The voyages of the

peace flotilla had hardly gone according to plan, but that did
not matter. 'Greenpeace' and 'Rainbow Warrior' had become
household words, and everyone in the South Pacific knew
what they stood for.

The trial in Auckland District Court of the 'Turenges',
Alain Mafart and Dominique Prieur, attracted a crowd of
journalists from New Zealand and overseas. They expected
the trial to last for weeks, during which time some of the
secrets of French intelligence operations were bound to be
revealed. As it happened, the appearance of the two prisoners
on 4 November was an anti-climax. By pleading guilty to a
reduced charge of manslaughter rather than innocent to a
charge of murder, the Turenges cut the trial short. No witnesses
were called, and within a couple of hours the French agents
were back in custody awaiting sentence. The New Zealand
government denied having done a deal with France to spare
Mitterrand political embarrassment. But even after 22 November,
when the Turenges were sentenced to 10 years' imprisonment,
the suspicion lingered that the two governments were co-
operating. A decent interval would elapse, people said, and
then the Turenges would be deported to France, where they
would receive a hero's welcome.

The sceptics were not far wrong. The New Zealand Prime
Minister David Lange boasted that justice was 'outside the
reach of government manipulation' in his country, and refused
repeated requests from Paris that the two agents be released.
But negotiations for a settlement between France and New
Zealand continued. Lange put himself in a difficult position.
Strong on rhetoric about justice, he soon realised that France
could make New Zealand pay dearly for sticking to principle.
While the Turenges sat in prison, the French government
embarked on a campaign of economic pressure against New
Zealand on their behalf. Never has a state done so much for
two terrorists.

French customs officers applied the letter of the law to
imports of New Zealand wool, opening bales for inspection
and disrupting the normal flow of business. French New
Caledonia stopped buying New Zealand lamb, and France
itself placed a ban on New Zealand sheep meat in the form of
brains. When the conservatives replaced the socialists as the

parliamentary French government in March 1986, Paris decided to touch an even more sensitive New Zealand nerve—exports to the whole of the European Economic Community. Since 1973, when Britain entered the EEC, New Zealand exports of butter to the region have fallen from 170 000 tonnes a year to less than 80 000 tonnes; and with the agreement covering such exports due to be renegotiated in August, France was in the position of being able to deal a heavy blow to the dairy farmers of New Zealand. Lange had no alternative but to reach a settlement.

Though it emerged as a compromise arbitrated by the Secretary-General of the UN, Xavier Perez de Cuellar, the settlement over the *Rainbow Warrior* affair was a victory for France and further evidence that the French intended to use their power against the small countries of the South Pacific. Jacques Chirac, the new French Prime Minister, conveyed the apologies of his country 'for the events which took place in Auckland on July 10 1985'. New Zealand received $7 million compensation and a guarantee of access for its butter to the EEC until 1989. But David Lange, who had once said that Alain Mafart and Dominique Prieur would not leave New Zealand during the term of his government, suffered the humiliation of seeing them deported after serving only eight months of their 10-year sentences. The agents were to spend the next three years on Hao atoll in French Polynesia, a support base for the nuclear tests at Moruroa. Here they would enjoy an enforced holiday under the palm trees and the tropical sun, in the company of fellow officers who regard them as noble patriots of the French Republic. And Mafart, once in charge of the Aspretto combat diving school in Corsica, would be able to practise his underwater skills in comfort. As the leader of the New Zealand Opposition, Jim Bolger, was quick to point out, it was hardly the fate which the New Zealand Prime Minister had promised for the spies from abroad. Bolger wanted to know whether the couple would be given 'suntan lotion, scuba gear and tennis rackets as a farewell gift from the New Zealand judicial system'. Not for sale in 1985, New Zealand justice sold in 1986 at the price of butter.

The French seizure of the *Vega* on 24 October 1985, encapsulated the clash of ideas which was at the heart of the *Rainbow*

Warrior affair. On one side was Admiral René Hugues, commander of the French Pacific Fleet, backed by President Mitterrand and Prime Minister Laurent Fabius in his determination to clear the Moruroa area of Greenpeace protesters. Fabius was actually at Moruroa to affirm the French stand. On the other side were the seven Greenpeace volunteers on board the *Vega*, waiting to be arrested by French commandos. The Greenpeace message, radioed before the seizure, was simple: 'We urgently appeal to France to cancel the test. We are fully aware of the risks we face, but the threat to the future of the people of the Pacific, posed by the release of radioactivity, is far greater.' Needless to say, the tests went ahead.

9

Moruroa

The bombing of the *Rainbow Warrior* damaged France's reputation throughout the South Pacific. As the Paris newspaper *Le Monde* said in April: 'A single year—1985—will doubtless have done as much for France's woes and misfortunes on the other side of the world as the preceding 100.'[1] In an attempt to restore its image and spread goodwill in the Island countries, France has now embarked on a public relations offensive of cultural exchanges and grants, its centrepiece being a new francophone university to be built in Tahiti and New Caledonia. Pacific Islanders, it is hoped, will feel better about the bomb as a result.

This latest twist in 20 years of French testing in the Pacific is a reminder that France has always employed two simple strategies to deal with opponents of the bomb, whether they are French colonial subjects or from other Pacific countries: it has either ignored them or tried to buy them off. The bomb itself has remained sacrosanct. Only in switching from atmospheric to underground testing in 1975 has France shown any respect for regional opinion.

For the French atomic test program to proceed in the 1960s, it was vital that French Polynesia remain firmly under the control of Paris. Independence and nuclear testing were irreconcilable, so independence was nipped in the bud. When the French started testing in the Pacific the best-known advocate of independence for the colony was Pouvanaa a Oopa, a leader whose appeal to the Polynesians was charismatic. But he was in a French gaol, sentenced to solitary confinement for eight years on a charge of having encouraged his followers to burn down Papeete, the capital; in fact, as everyone knew, he was imprisoned to keep him out of the way.

That left Pouvanaa's followers in French Polynesia in 1963 organised into two parties, the RDPT (Rassemblement Démocratique des Populations Tahitiennes) and the Tahitian Independence Party. The RDPT under John Teariki held a majority of seats in the local Territorial Assembly and was against the tests and for a time in favour of independence. But the powers of the Territorial Assembly were strictly limited. Even the draft of a bill asking for a referendum on nuclear testing was rejected by the governor as 'meddling in defence problems' and 'frankly political';[2] and when news reached Paris that the RDPT leaders in Tahiti proposed to hold a convention calling for independence, General de Gaulle simply dissolved the RDPT together with the Tahitian Independence Party. Once the armed forces and the French Atomic Energy Commission flooded into the territory and began to spend vast sums of money on firing bombs, people's living standards began to rise and their economic dependence on the presence of the military increased. The territory remains heavily subsidised by France today, importing far more than it exports. This subsidised standard of living, far higher in terms of cash than neighbouring countries such as the Cook Islands or Western Samoa, is the price France willingly pays for its nuclear test centre; and it is a price which has been high enough to weaken and contain, though by no means destroy, the independence movement.

With an energy which had never characterised civil construction in French Polynesia, the military rapidly covered Moruroa with nuclear installations, including two huge concrete blockhouses weighing 45 000 tonnes each to protect firing and measuring equipment. Thousands of foreign legionaries, army personnel and Atomic Energy Commission employees suddenly arrived in Tahiti during 1964, crowding into the small capital of Papeete, taking Tahitian women and provoking an upsurge of street violence.

The first bomb, with a 'small' yield of 25 to 30 kilotons, was exploded on a barge in Moruroa lagoon on 2 July 1966. A

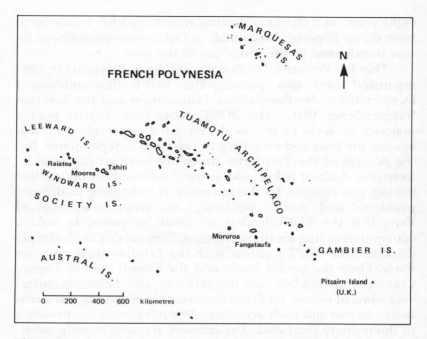

The Polynesians—70 per cent of the population 170 000—are at the bottom of the social pile in French Polynesia. Two small independence parties want the French to leave and call for an end to France's nuclear tests but France has bought off much opposition by pouring money into the colony.

few months later General de Gaulle visited French Polynesia. He was confronted by John Teariki, leader of the largest political party in the territory, and told to re-embark his troops, his bombs and his aeroplanes at once so that he would 'never be accused of having caused cancer and leukemia here in our islands'.[3] De Gaulle took no notice of this speech. Instead he insisted on observing a nuclear explosion on 11 September even though the wind was blowing the wrong way and distributed fallout over the people of French Polynesia, the Cook Islands, Samoa and Fiji. Having been delayed waiting for the wind to blow east, the General could wait no longer. He said to the nuclear men: 'I am proud and I am proud of you.'[4] In a diplomatic note New Zealand pointed to 'high levels of radioactivity in the air and in rainouts in various Pacific Islands, including the Cook Islands, Western Samoa and Fiji, following the detonations of 11 September and 4 October, 1966'.[5]

As the French tests continued, 29 in all between 1966 and 1972, the protests of neighbouring countries grew. The French insisted that all was well and that no one need be concerned in the least about fallout. But New Zealand's monitoring stations showed that each French explosion deposited significant fallout on the islands of the South Pacific. Sometimes westward winds blew back part of the radioactive cloud; mostly the cloud circled the earth in an easterly direction, leaving its debris throughout the southern hemisphere. Australian scientists made similar observations on the Australian continent, where the French bombs caused increased concentrations of iodine−131 in milk and a sharp rise in contamination by strontium−90 and calcium−137. New Zealand and Australia therefore called for an end to French testing. During the nine years of protest by Australia up to 1973, France did not deign to reply on a single occasion and it was only after the election of the Whitlam Labor government that a French response was at last forthcoming.

The years 1972 and 1973 marked a sharp intensification of South Pacific protests against French testing. Demonstrators took to the streets in Australia and New Zealand, French airline offices in several Australian cities were attacked and the government of newly independent Fiji banned all French military or naval aircraft and shipping from using its facilities. The Australian Council of Trade Unions, led by Bob Hawke, placed bans on the movement of French goods through Australian ports and blocked mail to and from France. The Liberal Prime Minister William MacMahon was condemned for not making stronger representations to the French about the tests. Embarrassed, he joined with New Zealand in a joint approach to the UN Committee on Disarmament asking that the tests be stopped.

The timid and respectful diplomatic notes sent to France by conservative governments in Australia and New Zealand had achieved nothing except perhaps to earn the scorn of the French. The new Labor governments of Gough Whitlam and Norman Kirk, elected at the end of 1972, were more aggressive, imaginative and effective. Both Prime Ministers quickly initiated talks with the French insisting that the tests stop.

When the talks produced no result and the French government announced in May 1973 that it would go on testing regardless of opinion in Australia and New Zealand, Whitlam and Kirk took France to the International Court of Justice in the Hague seeking a Court order to bring the tests to an end. France refused to recognise the jurisdiction of the Court, and no French representative appeared before it. But the case received worldwide publicity, and that was what Australia and New Zealand wanted.

New Zealand complained that French testing was a 'gross invasion' of the rights and liberties of New Zealanders and other South Pacific peoples: 'The people of New Zealand, the Cook Islands, Niue and the Tokelau Islands actively resent the contamination of the air they breathe and of the waters from which their food supplies are drawn ... It is an obvious imposition that it should be necessary to maintain in New Zealand itself, and in the Pacific Islands, outposts to keep watch on the fluctuating levels of an unnatural and unsought hazard.' To contaminate the atmosphere with radioactive fall-out, New Zealand said, was 'pernicious and inexcusable'.[6] Australia argued similarly: fallout infringed national sovereignty and subjected Australians to an insidious and unavoidable poison which invaded 'people's bones and lungs and critical body organs'; ionising radiation was known to be harmful to human life. Addressing the Court in the Hague on 21 May 1973 Senator Lionel Murphy, for Australia, pointed out that 'for infants who feed on fresh cows' milk derived from one major Australian milk production area, the dose commitments to their thyroids in the seven-year period, 1966 to 1972, of French nuclear weapon testing in the atmosphere in the Pacific ranged up to the equivalent of approximately three years' additional exposure to natural background radiation. Can there be any wonder that this concerns the Australian Government and creates anxiety among the Australian people?'[7]

The case extended over 18 months while learned judges called for more evidence on whether the International Court of Justice could make a decision in the dispute. In the interim the Court ordered on 22 June 1973 that France should not aggravate the dispute by continuing to test nuclear weapons. The French ignored the order, exploding two bombs at the

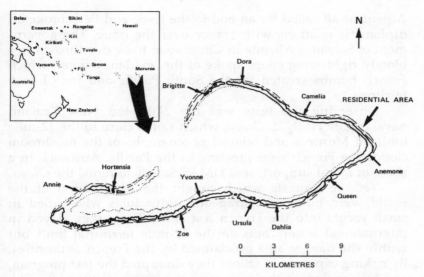

Moruroa Atoll, the visible rim of an extinct volcano, has sunk more than 1.5 metres since French testing went underground in 1975. The code-names are for atoll zones, most of which have been sites for nuclear tests. Since 1966 the French have exploded more than 110 nuclear bombs at Moruroa, 41 of them in the atmosphere.

end of July and another on 19 August. When Australia protested, France's reply was to detonate two more bombs on 24 and 29 August.

In French Polynesia itself the 1973 tests were the focus of unprecedented public opposition. An anti-bomb rally organised by the radical French politician and publicist Jean-Jacques Servan-Schreiber in the capital of Papeete attracted more than 5000 people, mostly Polynesians, who marched through the streets with anti-nuclear placards. A French pastor, Gilbert Nicolas, conducted a hunger strike for 22 days. The autonomist leaders Francis Sanford and Pouvaana used the occasion of the nuclear tests to call for a referendum on independence. Nothing happened as a result because all important decisions about French Polynesia continued to be made in Paris, not Papeete.

Latin American countries also registered their disapproval of the 1973 tests. Chile, Ecuador, Colombia, Venezuela and

Argentina all called for an end to the tests, and Peru broke off diplomatic relations with France over the issue. The government of Salvador Allende in Chile, soon to be overthrown in a bloody right-wing coup, spoke of the 'evident danger' which French bombs created for the South Pacific and for Chilean territory.

Observing the tests was the 24000-ton New Zealand naval frigate HMNZS *Otago*, which sailed close to the 12-mile limit off Moruroa and relayed photographs of the mushroom clouds the French were creating in the Pacific. Australia, in a show of moral support, sent HMAS *Supply* to refuel the *Otago*.

Yet the protests which caught the imagination of the world were those of courageous individuals who sailed in small yachts into the French test zone. There they stayed in international waters outside the 12-mile territorial limit but within the danger area proclaimed by the French authorities. By risking exposure to fallout they disrupted the test program, and by positioning themselves on the high seas they offered a dramatic challenge to France's claim that it could unilaterally abolish the freedom of the seas over tens of thousands of square kilometres of ocean. Governments can easily dispatch notes of protest from the comfortable offices of foreign affairs bureaucracies. They can pay lawyers to appear at the Hague. They can send the Navy to take pictures. It is another matter entirely to spend months at sea on a small sailing vessel in cramped quarters, cut off from the outside world by French radio jamming devices, hounded by French naval patrols and unsure whether anyone cares what you are doing. This was the experience of the Canadian David McTaggart, a former businessman, who first confronted the French in their nuclear lair when he sailed *Greenpeace III* from New Zealand to Moruroa in 1972.

For weeks the *Greenpeace III* hove-to off Moruroa, ignoring instructions from the admiral commanding the nuclear tests force to withdraw to a safe distance, and being harassed by the French Navy. The presence of *Greenpeace III* undoubtedly delayed the testing program, and in exasperation, the French finally rammed the small sailing boat with one of their mine-sweepers. They took McTaggart and his two companions a-shore on Moruroa, stage-managed a friendly lunch with the admiral for the sake of favourable publicity, made hasty repairs to *Greenpeace III* and sent McTaggart on his way. In the international press they depicted the incident as McTaggart's fault, a collision at sea to which they had responded with help and hospitality. The French version of events was false but it sounded convincing. France denied responsibility for the damage to *Greenpeace III* and the Canadian government offered McTaggart no assistance of any value.

By the time McTaggart set sail for the French test zone in 1973, however, things had changed. The voyages of small sailing boats to French Polynesia had become a popular symbol of resisting France's nuclear tests. Other boats such as the 30-metre former Baltic trader *Fri* and the nine-metre sloop *Carmen* sailed across the Pacific to the Tuamotus. *Greenpeace III*, leaving late in June, covered three thousand miles in 21 days. In her diary crew member Anne-Marie Horne wrote of the voyage: 'Generally, everything is moving. Have to be always bracing oneself. Wind howling non-stop. Water slushing and crashing. One bruise after another. Everything damp today. Each time we come about, anything that is loose crashes to the other side. Mary and I aren't allowed to eat anything ... Exhausting.'[8]

This time the French did not hesitate to take action against *Greenpeace III*. When it reached the sea west of the mouth of Moruroa lagoon the French Navy sent a boarding party to make arrests even though the vessel was outside the 12-mile limit. McTaggart has described his treatment by the French sailors: 'The first truncheon came down with a weight and force unlike anything I had ever felt on the back of my head and the second came down across my shoulders and the next blow landed on the back of my neck and the next on my head again and the next on my spine and the next on my shoulder blade and the next against my kidney and I was suddenly in the air being flipped over the railing and being yanked furiously into the inflatable, unable to catch a single breath or even find a way to make a sound.'[9] McTaggart's right eye was a mass of bloody pulp. His companion Nigel Ingram was kicked in the groin and knocked unconscious. But at great personal risk Anne-Marie Horne was able to smuggle film of the French assaults out of French Polynesia. Published around the world, the photographs caused a storm of protest. A month before, the French had boarded the *Fri*, whose crew included a group of French 'peace commandos'. New Zealand protested formally on both occasions, stating that it refused to accept that the French Government had any right to suspend international navigation on the high seas, and complaining of the illegal arrest of New Zealand citizens. The Canadian Prime Minister, Pierre Trudeau, presented the French Ambassador with a stern rebuke. McTaggart returned to Vancouver a hero.

The voyages of *Greenpeace III* and the other yachts into the test zone dramatised the nuclear issue in French Polynesia in a uniquely effective way. They undoubtedly played a crucial role in arousing world opinion against France and compelling the French to move their tests underground. Towards the end of 1973 the French began to talk openly of conducting tests beneath the surface of the earth and, after the elections of mid-1974, the new President Giscard d'Estaing announced that France would be in a position to move to the stage of underground firings as soon as the tests series scheduled for that summer had been completed.[10] As if to prove that no one could push France around, a final series of blasts in the atmosphere deposited radioactive fallout throughout the southern hemisphere in 1974. The bombing of the *Rainbow Warrior* in 1985 must be seen as the climax of a long period of French irritation with the environmentalist activities of the Greenpeace organisation, beginning in 1972.

Once *les bombes* began to go off in test pits hundreds of metres under the ground rather than in the air, objections to the tests subsided. The judges of the International Court of Justice dropped the cases brought by Australia and New Zealand on the grounds that a dispute no longer existed. And for a few years little was heard about the nuclear tests in the Pacific except that they were still taking place, though the autonomist deputy from French Polynesia, Francis Sanford, had the foresight to ask the French government in 1975 whether 'it is not to be feared that repeated nuclear explosions in the base of these atolls may result in an accumulation of radioactive elements and their gradual diffusion into the ocean environment through the porous rock of which they are formed'.[11]

The point of Sanford's question was illustrated by a serious accident which occurred at Moruroa on 25 July 1979. As technicians lowered a bomb down an 800-metre shaft it jammed. They could not move it up or down. So they took a chance and exploded the bomb where it was. Soon afterwards seismographs in New Zealand and the Cook Islands recorded the largest earth tremor ever from Moruroa, and within a couple of hours a tidal wave swept over the atoll. Though the French authorities have never admitted any connection between the bomb and the tidal wave, the blast probably loosened a chunk of the porous outer wall of the atoll under-water or caused the collapse of an underground cave, releasing radioactive substances into the surrounding sea.

Revelations made in 1981 by a French trade union whose members work on Moruroa, the Confédération Française Démocratique du Travail, support this interpretation: 'In 1979, the explosion of a bomb blasted out a piece from the under-lying crater. This produced a spectacular tidal wave which carried off some shelters. As a precaution for the future, a seismograph was installed and was connected to a whistle which was supposed to warn us if a similar accident happened during or after another bomb explosion. At the same time, platforms resting on posts and surrounded by hand-rails were built for the use of the personnel during the tests and as a refuge from tidal waves. Each platform can hold 500 persons.'[12] In another accident in 1979, described by the authorities as non-nuclear, two people were killed and four injured by an explosion in a concrete chamber for the study of shockwaves. According to the journalist Jean d'Arriulat of *Le Matin*, the treatment of the injured workers suggested that they had been contaminated with radioactivity. Nurses looking after them wore gloves. Doctors were specially protected from their patients. On Moruroa, it is alleged, the accident created a radioactive cloud. Forty technicians were flown from France solely for the purpose of decontaminating areas of the atoll.[13] Because of the strict military secrecy surrounding every aspect of France's testing program, the full truth about these accidents may never be known.

With its limited powers, the Territorial Assembly in Tahiti was unable to investigate the accidents properly. It adopted unanimously a resolution saying: 'We are unable to accept the sacrifice of human lives in the conducting of uncontrollable tests.'[14] It called for a team of impartial experts to make a study of Moruroa, and for the establishment of a permanent monitoring laboratory. But all the Assembly got from the government of Giscard d'Estaing was a visiting mission led by the head of the French Atomic Energy Commission, Jean Teillac, and a brief trip for six Assembly members to a part of the atoll well away from where the accidents happened. The Assembly members could not even find out the names of workers, far less details of their injuries.

The evidence given by trade unionists and engineers working on Moruroa now make it possible to piece together a far more realistic picture of French testing than has ever been offered in the anodyne statements of officials. For a number of years surface plutonium was fixed to the ground by mixing it with tar. At the same time a garbage dump of contaminated scrap iron, wood, plastic and clothing accumulated at the western tip of the atoll. When a large storm hit Moruroa on 22 March 1981 pounding seas swept the garbage and the plutonium-impregnated tar into the lagoon. Some reached the open ocean. Other refuse was deposited on beaches around the atoll, only to be redistributed by another storm in August. Furthermore, engineers claim that Moruroa sinks with each nuclear explosion and sank more than 1.5 metres between 1975 and 1981. Cracks have appeared on islands of the atoll, and are clearly shown on an army map of June 1980.[15] The charge that Moruroa is like a radioactive sponge, constantly contaminating the surrounding seas, cannot be dismissed.

If optimists in the South Pacific expected the election of François Mitterrand as President of France in 1981 to bring the tests to an end, they were quickly disillusioned. Mitterrand raised people's hopes in the Pacific only to dash them again. As soon as he became President he ordered that the nuclear tests be suspended while the new Socialist government conducted a thorough review of the issue. The review, one of the speediest made by any government, was over in four days. Its conclusion was that the tests should continue as before. Perhaps the truth of the matter is that no French government, in particular a Socialist one, can govern without the support of the Army and the officer corps. The only change at Moruroa after the election of Mitterrand was that the commanding admiral was instructed to release at least some information to the people of the Territory. The result was an official admission, for the first time, that 'some of the nuclear waste left by the atmospheric explosions made before 1975, may have crossed the lagoon to the eastern side of the atoll'.[16] Previously nuclear waste had not officially existed at Moruroa.

As in 1972, the coming to power of a Labor government in Australia in 1983 put French testing in the headlines again. The Hawke government not only protested against the resumption of testing at Moruroa on 20 April; it also announced that, in line with Labor policy, Australia would promote the establishment of a nuclear free zone in the South Pacific. The French Embassy in Canberra issued a statement claiming that radioactivity in the air and seawater in French Polynesia were carefully monitored and that, far from cancer being more common there than elsewhere, people in Tahiti and other parts of the territory actually contracted cancer less frequently than people in Australia, New Zealand and France.[17] The bomb is good for you, the French Embassy seemed to be saying. As critics were quick to point out, the French cancer statistics were woefully inadequate. They showed only the cases treated in the Mamao government hospital and another small hospital in Papeete, and omitted the hospital on Moruroa itself. Quite apart from that, as anyone familiar with French Polynesia would know, many villagers die on the numerous remote islands of the territory without ever consulting a doctor. As for the argument that radioactive levels are carefully checked, the important point is that the checking is done by those with a vested interest in presenting optimistic reports, the Army and the Atomic Energy Commission. France's independent National Radiation Laboratory has not been allowed to make studies.

At the invitation of the French government, six scientists from Australia, New Zealand and Papua New Guinea spent four days at Moruroa in 1983. Their task was to investigate radioactive contamination of the atoll environment and examine health statistics for the population of French Polynesia, and their findings are known as the Atkinson Report after the

New Zealand radiation expert who led the team.[18] The trip was a good example of scientists blundering into a political trap. Whatever the scientists said was sure to be expressed in the qualified and arcane language of scholarship, inaccessible to the general public and therefore interpreted by politicians with axes to grind, French politicians above all. As the government of Vanuatu warned beforehand, France would use the Atkinson Report to justify its nuclear tests; and so it has. After his visit to Moruroa in September 1985, President Mitterrand renewed his offer to scientists to examine the atoll, saying the Atkinson report had already shown that the tests 'are harmless, that there is no danger'.[19]

The Atkinson Report certainly let the French off lightly. It said that the nuclear tests had not created a danger to health from radiation in the atmosphere at Moruroa; the atoll might eventually leak radioactive materials into the ocean but not for more than 500 years; and the management of radioactive waste at the test site, once poor, was now very good. All of this sounded like the last word on the subject until people started reading the report more carefully. The military, it turned out, had imposed restrictions on where the scientists went and what evidence they collected. They were not permitted to go to the northern part of the atoll where accidents occurred in 1979 and 1981. Instead they inspected part of the southern margin and saw the rest from a plane. Nor were they allowed to see the cracks caused by testing or obtain samples of coral from within the lagoon in order to assess the degree of contamination by plutonium. On the question of fissures in the volcanic rock where the explosions occur, the report admitted that 'key post-test data were not made available for inspection.'[20]

By comparison with the painstaking and lengthy fieldwork undertaken by the Laboratory of Radiation Biology of the University of Washington during the American tests of the 1950s, when scientists regularly spent months collecting land and sea samples and had the full co-operation of the US Navy, the Atkinson team's four days under the watchful eyes of the French seem ludicrously inadequate. Unsurprisingly, experts in marine geology have challenged its findings. Matthias Tomczak of the Marine Studies Centre at the University of

Sydney points out that the visitors to Moruroa say nothing about the risks of future tests. The director of Auckland's geothermal institute, Manfred Hochstein, thinks the Atkinson report is wrong in its explanation of why Moruroa atoll has subsided since underground tests began. In his view, short-term leakage of radionuclides into the ocean might well be taking place already; fresh explosions will 'probably increase the permeability of other parts of the atoll and leakage will be enhanced in the near future, especially if bores in the lagoon are used for future testing'.[21]

The *Centre d'Expérimentation du Pacifique* dominates French Polynesia. The bomb has systematically skewed the economy of the colony into a kind of nuclear dependency, in which exports cover about six per cent of foreign purchases and the difference is made up by money from Paris. The bomb has brought hospitals, schools and television sets but it has also created festering slums in the capital of Papeete. Many Polynesians who were recruited from the outlying islands during the construction phase are now unemployed and eke out an existence among the rats and open sewers of the shanties. While the Chinese, the French and the mixed-race community have done well out of the bomb, the Polynesians— about 70 per cent of the population of 170000—stay at the bottom of the social pile. The image of Tahiti conveyed by tourist brochures is one of Polynesian charm, hospitality and sensual ease, recalling the paintings of Gauguin. In reality, 'Tahiti is little more than a vast supply base for the nuclear program' and many Tahitians live in urban shacks or crowded apartment blocks.[22] The traditions of the Polynesians are fast being lost.

Yet France has little to fear from disaffection within French Polynesia. The Evangelical Church, which claims the allegiance of the majority of Polynesians, opposes nuclear testing and wants a referendum on the issue. Two political parties stand for independence and an end to testing. But in the 1986 territorial elections the ruling pro-French party, *Teuiraa Tahoeraa*, which has strong links with the conservative *Rassemblement pour la République* in France, confirmed its hold on power with a majority of 24 to 17. *Tahoeraa* benefited from its influence over newspapers, radio and television in the colony, and from its ability to dispense jobs and favours. The pro-independence parties won only five seats out of 41: three went to Jacqui Drollet's *la mana te nunaa* ('let the people have the power') and two to Oscar Temaru's Polynesian Liberation Front, which has growing support from the slum-dwellers of Papeete. For the independence leaders, decolonisation of French Polynesia offers the only hope of bringing nuclear tests to an end. Drollet sees 'the will of colonised peoples to become independent and control their own destinies fully' as the 'only force that ever could stop ... French nuclear tests ...'[23]

Even if the independence movement should one day succeed, France holds a final trumpcard. Legally speaking, Moruroa and Fangataufa atolls are integral parts of France itself. They were ceded to the French Republic in 1964 by an obscure vote in the Territorial Assembly in Tahiti.

10

Why the French love
the bomb

Throughout the melodrama of the *Rainbow Warrior* affair few
stopped to ask why France has nuclear weapons in the first
place. Why should France give the Soviet Union greater incentive than it already has to train missiles at French targets?

Since 1958 when France decided to acquire a nuclear capability, the French justification for this policy has remained the
same: only countries with nuclear arms 'are really able to meet
all the possible risks to their security and independence';
French nuclear arms would be used only to defend French
territory; the Americans are unreliable allies who will sacrifice
Europe, if need be, to save themselves. Pierre Mauroy, President
Mitterrand's first Prime Minister, said in 1982: 'Deterrence for
France was made feasible by the equalizing power of the
atom. The purpose of deterrence is to prevent war by convincing a would-be aggressor that a major action against France
would present unacceptable risks with regard to the political
aims he is pursuing. Under our strategy of defence by the
weak against the strong, France's strategic nuclear forces have
the capacity, even after an enemy first strike, to retaliate with
a very high degree of credibility and to inflict damage in
excess of the demographic and economic potential we present.'[1]
French strategists believe that their nuclear weapons are more
likely to deter war in Europe than those of the USA because
the Russians would never doubt France's determination to
push the button.

The French Ambassador in Canberra told Australia in
1973 that France's decision to acquire nuclear weapons was

'divorced from any empty considerations of prestige, and inspired by the purely defensive concern of deterring any possible aggressor'.[2] In fact prestige matters a great deal to the French. They think their nuclear weapons add to their prestige. They take pride in being one of the five nuclear-armed nations. They stress their absolute rights of sovereignty in the Pacific. They take offence at criticism of their testing program, which they believe makes them a great nation. Moruroa has become a symbol of France's determination to assert its national independence in a world dominated by the two superpowers, and far from leaving the Pacific the French plan to intensify their colonial and military presence there. The more French defence strategy hinges on nuclear rather than conventional forces, the more vital French Polynesia becomes.

New Caledonia, the other main French territory in the Pacific, is also gaining in strategic importance. In 1985 the *Rubis* became the first French nuclear submarine to visit New Caledonia and more will be coming. Port Denouel in Noumea harbour is the site of a new military base, one which will service the growing fleet of French aircraft carriers and nuclear submarines, and construction of the base is proceeding in spite of the tension over independence for the territory. Acquired by France as a penal colony in 1853, New Caledonia is today torn by an independence struggle between the original Melanesian inhabitants, the Kanaks, and the mainly French settlers who outnumber them. After disturbances between white settlers and Kanaks of the Kanak Socialist National Liberation Front (FLNKS) a state of emergency was declared in January 1985. It lasted six months, during which time even the presence of 5000 soldiers and gendarmes could not prevent hostilities.

The Socialist government responded to the emergency with a complex arrangement splitting New Caledonia into four regions, each with direct links to Paris. In the territorial elections of October 1985 the pro-independence FLNKS gained control of three regions, the central, the north and the Loyalty Islands, while the anti-independence forces won the largely white right-wing town of Noumea. The Socialists had intended New Caledonia to proceed eventually to a form of semi-autonomy. But the conservative Chirac government which won the French parliamentary elections in 1986 moved quickly to block any kind of independence for the colony, by stripping the regions of their powers and opposing electoral reform. Under a policy known as 'nomadisation', thousands of French troops were dispersed throughout the country so as to prevent the FLNKS from mobilising. The French Army followed a similar policy in Algeria.[3] The referendum on the political future of the territory, due to take place before mid-1987, has been designed to ensure that France wins. The FLNKS will boycott it. The colonial status of the territory was recognised in a UN vote of December 1986, which put New Caledonia back on the list of non-selfgoverning territories.

In New Caledonia, as elsewhere in the Pacific Islands, the nuclear presence and colonialism go together. Colonies must achieve independence before they can be nuclear free. An independent Republic of Kanaky governed by the FLNKS would almost certainly follow the examples of Vanuatu and New Zealand and refuse port access to nuclear vessels, whereas New Caledonia either as a French territory or as an associated francophone state would welcome such vessels. The new French base at Noumea, hailed by Charles Hernu on his visit to the Pacific a few months before he was forced to resign as Defence Minister, is incontrovertible evidence that France, even under a Socialist government, had no intention of granting genuine independence to its Melanesian colony. The Chirac government is unashamedly determined to lock that colony more firmly into the French imperial orbit. In the future as in the past these little bits of France on the other side of the world are supposed to do their duty by serving the strategic interests of the Motherland.

The *Rainbow Warrior* scandal erupted at a politically sensitive time for the French military, which is engaged in a major effort to modernise and increase its nuclear forces. Indeed the Socialist François Mitterrand oversees a rapid and massive nuclear build-up. Strategists distinguish between two types of nuclear-weapon systems, 'strategic' and 'tactical'. If war were actually to be fought with nuclear arms the distinction would probably be meaningless because of rapid escalation of the conflict, but in theory the 'strategic' weapons would be used only in dire emergency. They are the long-range weapons capable of reaching enemy territory directly from France or, in the case of missiles, launched from submarines in oceans and seas such as the Atlantic and the Mediterranean; their payloads are the most destructive of nuclear bombs. 'Tactical' weapons are fired over shorter distances and carry less powerful, though still devastating, explosive devices. In the fanciful scenarios of the strategists, tactical weapons are reserved for 'battlefield' use in the belief that nuclear conflict could be confined to limited geographical areas. For the French, the assumed battlefield is West Germany, just as for the Americans the battle would take place in Western Europe.

The single aim of a nuclear weapons system is to deliver a bomb to its target. Bombs can be carried in aircraft and dropped, as they were in the Second World War. The present force of French Mirage IV bombers, which went into service in 1964, represents this kind of method. But almost all bombs or 'warheads' are now designed to be carried by rockets, universally referred to as missiles, which can be fired from holes in the ground, aircraft, submarines, tanks or even trucks which move around the countryside. A confusing array of acronyms, such as SLBM, IRBM, MIRV and ASMP, are used to describe different kinds of missiles and different ways of taking a nuclear bomb to where it will be exploded. What is important in the French case is that France is modernising every kind of weapon system with the single exception of dropping bombs from Mirage IVs, which are due to be replaced by mobile missiles in the mid-1990s.

Even in 1980, according to an official report, French nuclear strategic forces were 'capable of killing 20 million individuals, wounding an equivalent number, and causing major disorganization of enemy activities nationwide'.[4] Their ability to kill will be many times greater in ten years' time, and so will that of the tactical forces. The number of strategic warheads, 132 in 1983, will be 692 by the mid-1990s; nuclear submarines will carry more than seven times as many warheads (592 compared with 80); and tactical warheads will increase from 153 to 238. Altogether France will possess a mighty arsenal of death by about 1995, at least 930 nuclear bombs in all, which together will be able to lay waste much of the Soviet Union.

The Pluton short-range missiles, first deployed by France in 1974, will begin to be replaced in 1992 by the Hades, which goes further, can be fired from French national territory to reach eastern Europe, is fitted with a larger bomb and will therefore kill more people if used. France may decide to equip some Hades missiles with the neutron bomb, that ultimate refinement of the inhuman logic of nuclearisation, a weapon which kills human beings with intense doses of radiation while leaving property intact. At present eighteen S−3 missiles, each ready to carry a one-megaton bomb a distance of 3500 kilometres, sit in concrete holes in the ground on the Albion Plateau in south-eastern France; all could be launched within seven minutes. Under the nuclear modernisation program the French plan to deploy a new intermediate range missile called the SX. By 1996 as many as 100 SX missiles will be ready to be fired from their trucks or 'transporter-erector-launchers' at targets 4000 kilometres away in the Soviet Union.

The special prestige of the Navy is shown by the fact that the centrepiece of France's nuclear deterrent is the French Oceanic Strategic Force, consisting of six nuclear submarines. Each is powered by a nuclear reactor using enriched uranium and is equipped with 16 ballistic missiles, which would be fired from tubes in the event of war. Under the modernisation program the present generation of missiles, M−20s with a range of about 3000 kilometres, will be replaced by more deadly and versatile weapons called M−4s. Not only is the M−4 capable of travelling a greater distance but it will carry six nuclear bombs programmed to hit six different targets. The striking power of France's *Redoutable*-class submarines and of a completely new class of submarines due to be introduced in 1994 is being increased far beyond that of any other part of the nuclear forces. In the understated words of General Lacaze, there will be a 'significant augmentation of our numbers of weapons ... throughout the next 20 years'.[5] France is determined not to be outdone by the superpowers. Expecting both the USA and the Soviet Union to have Star Wars missile defences in space, the French Defence Minister announced in 1985 that France would develop miniature nuclear warheads capable of penetrating such anti-missile shields.[6]

The French are encouraged to feel protected by their bomb

and to believe that it makes France a sanctuary, while in fact the $30 billion to be spent on nuclear modernisation in the next decade will only ensure that the Russians target France more comprehensively than ever. Despite all the talk from Paris about French independence, Moscow knows that French missiles point east. They are an addition to the Western nuclear arms build-up, and no Western European leader has been a more enthusiastic supporter of the deployment of American cruise and Pershing II missiles in Europe than President Mitterrand. The expansion of the French nuclear arsenal will provoke a matching response from the Soviet Union, which has never failed to respond to arms competition from the Americans. While France may not be in NATO, it is still part of the Atlantic Alliance and seen by Moscow as an ally of the Americans. The most important effect of France's nuclear build-up will be to complicate arms control negotiations and make agreement between the superpowers on limiting nuclear weapons more difficult to reach than ever. The second consequence is that the French military will come to rely more and more on nuclear rather than conventional methods of warfare. One of the attractions of nuclear weapons for France is that, in the mad world of defence expenditure, they are relatively cheap. Missiles cost less than men, and the armed forces' manpower will have dropped by 35 000 in the five years to 1988. But the rundown in conventional forces leaves commanders with fewer non-nuclear alternatives in the event of conflict. Horrible as ordinary war is, it remains far preferable to Armageddon.

Most French people are in favour of the bomb. A peace movement exists in France, led by the *Mouvement de la paix*, but this organisation is linked to the French Communist Party which favours France's nuclear force. Apart from the *Mouvement de la paix*, peace groups are small, numerous, ideological and uninfluential. There is no equivalent of Britain's Campaign for Nuclear Disarmament (CND) to unite competing factions under a single banner or indeed of the political culture of moral anti-militarism which sustains CND. In France 'it is quite possible to be on the Left and not opposed to the army, colonialism, or the atom bomb'.[7] General de Gaulle established the nuclear force in 1960. Nuclear bombs began

exploding in the South Pacific in 1966. The Left at first ob-
jected. Communists, Socialists and radical republicans alike
were united in opposing the entire nuclear project. During the
1965 Presidential campaign Mitterrand promised to ban the
force de frappe. The following year he said there was 'no more
terrible danger to the survival of the human species' than
the nuclear bomb. 'What France wants for herself, Israel and
Egypt, India and Pakistan will want for themselves and
Germany in its turn, and all the states of the earth. We must
not hesitate to proclaim it: the proliferation of nuclear arms
leads to the extension of conflicts.'[8]

In the 1974 Presidential election, which he lost narrowly
to Giscard d'Estaing, Mitterrand said he did not think the
tests at Moruroa were necessary and he would stop them if
elected. By this time Mitterrand was standing as the candidate
of the Union of the Left, which embraced Communists and
Left Radicals as well as Socialists. The policy agreed in the
Left's Common Programme in 1972 was to renounce the 'strategic nuclear strike force in any form', halt testing immediately
and sign the test ban treaty as first steps towards general
disarmament. Swords were to be beaten into ploughshares in
a plan by which the nuclear arms industry would be converted
to peaceful use.

Never a firm coalition, the Union of the Left crumbled
and finally fell apart in 1977. The parties reconsidered their
policies. Without any debate inside the party, the Central
Committee of the French Communist Party performed an ideological reversal in May 1977 by suddenly accepting that nuclear weapons were 'the only means of real deterrence available'.[9] Faithful Communist voters were reassured by a defence
policy which called for French missiles to be pointed not
merely at the Russians but in all directions, though no one
asked why intermediate-range S−2 missiles should face
the USA yet be capable of reaching only halfway across the
Atlantic. It was a comforting fiction for French Communists to
believe that, in their hands, France would be evenhandedly
nuclear and that its missiles would threaten both the superpowers rather than just the Soviet Union. In fact, ever since
the French nuclear force was formed it has threatened only
one country, the Soviet Union.

In the bitter public wrangling which followed the break-up of the Union of the Left the Communists accused the Socialists of not supporting independent national defence for France. But the Socialists were not far behind in abandoning their reservations about nuclear arms. The left wing of the Socialist party, represented by Jean-Pierre Chevènement's Centre for Socialist Study, Research and Education (CERES), took the initiative in pushing the party in a strongly pro-nuclear direction. After a period of hesitation when they talked of keeping the submarines while getting rid of the land-based missiles and the nuclear bombers, the Socialists turned full circle and became enthusiastic advocates of rapidly modernising all weapons systems. They now argue that a truly independent French nuclear force will keep the peace in Europe: the USA and the Soviet Union have assured their own security but have made the possibility of war in Europe more likely; safe at home, they will be tempted to fight on European soil and can be deterred only by a strong nuclear France.

The contrast between France and other European countries on the nuclear issue is striking. While West Germany, the Netherlands and Britain were convulsed by protests and demonstrations against the deployment in Western Europe of new American missiles in the first half of the 1980s, France was quiet. The French press depicted the peace movements as instruments of the Soviet Union. No public debate about nuclear strategy has taken place in France. President Mitterrand has been Reagan's greatest supporter in Europe. The tradition of French anti-establishment activism is weakening. As if to confirm what the French sociologist Alain Touraine calls 'the profound deterioration of French political life', the sinking of the *Rainbow Warrior* by French spies provoked hardly a single protest in France.[10]

How is this to be explained? Why does the French Left support the bomb and why is the peace movement in France so weak? The fundamental answer is that the bomb is French, not foreign, and has become a symbol of France's independence from the superpowers. The appeal of nationalism, of pride in the achievements of the French nation, is as compelling for people on the Left as it is for those on the Right. Incredible as it may seem to us who live in the South Pacific, the Left still cherishes a belief in France's uniquely progressive role in world history. Chevènement, for example, was able to excite his colleagues in the Socialist Party with a vision of France audaciously breaking with the capitalist system and creating socialism in the heart of the developed world, a political project which could be realised only if France had its own nuclear force and was therefore under no obligation to the Americans. The gap between this inspiring rhetoric and the dreary reality of the Mitterrand government yawns wide. Mitterrand himself sees France as the champion of small countries and for a while supplied arms to the Sandinistas in Nicaragua in order to help them in their struggle against American-backed counter-revolutionaries. He defends human rights in Central America and explodes bombs in Polynesia. What has happened is that Gaullism in defence policy, the idea that France shall bow to no one in deciding how to defend itself, has won large sections of Left opinion. The bomb has triumphed because of its nationality.

The Left is pro-nuclear for other reasons. Left intellectuals in France generally regard purely moral arguments against the bomb as naive and see themselves as realists in a hard world. They share with their compatriots the collective French memory of the German occupation during the Second World War. They want no repetition of Munich, appeasement and defeat. Distrust of the Soviet Union is an attitude which the French Left now displays with pride, the Communists in order to establish their credentials as true Eurocommunists free from Moscow's influence, and the Socialists in order to prove that they are not Communists. Nowhere in Western Europe was there such enthusiasm for Polish Solidarity and its struggle against the Russians as in France.

All French governments must favour the bomb in order to survive. Gaullism in defence policy has become a vital element in the French political consensus, something all the major political forces agree upon. No government of the French Republic, which for two centuries has experienced periodic ruptures of the political order, wants to undermine that consensus; and so the State, the conservative civil service and the usually patriotic news media combine to keep the people happy with nuclear weapons. Nor can any government ignore the Army, whose loyalty is a precondition of political stability. That loyalty cannot be relied upon unless the officer corps gets what it wants. As one general said in the midst of the *Rainbow Warrior* scandal in 1985, if the Socialist government were to punish the military for the bungle in New Zealand, there would be a 'malaise' in the Army. In the words of John Ralston Saul, this is 'a process by which the French Army distances itself from the existing regime, undermines public confidence in elected officials and, periodically, brings the government down'. It is 'a highly sophisticated form of *coup d'état*'.[11] The Army brought down the French regime in 1958 and was involved in an attempt to assassinate General de Gaulle in 1961.

Although the political influence of the French Army is now counter-balanced by a well-armed *gendarmerie* loyal to the government, Mitterrand and his ministers ran in fear of the Army in their handling of the *Rainbow Warrior* affair. The Socialists had, after all, spent years of patient work in the 1970s convincing the generals that a left-wing government did not threaten them; and Charles Hernu, former Defence minister, has always been a friend of the military. That is why he told lies about *Rainbow Warrior* until he was forced to resign, and why he was rehabilitated and decorated with the *Légion d'Honneur* in 1986. Too proud to tolerate criticism and too powerful to be offended, the French armed forces, the Army in particular, emerged from the bungle of the *Rainbow Warrior* affair in a strengthened condition. In desperate attempts to placate them, the Socialist government placed the secret services under direct Army control for the first time since 1971 and revived a discredited regiment, the 11th Shock, which de Gaulle disbanded in 1962 because of its collaboration with the officers who tried to kill him. The 11th Shock Regiment, with its extreme right-wing tradition, is under the command of Colonel Jean-Claude Lesquer, who played an important part in organising the bombing in New Zealand; it has assumed responsibility for training soldiers for the DGSE Action Division and it has taken over the frogmen's school in Corsica.[12]

Of course, a minority of the French will always be sceptical. A poll conducted for *Le Matin* in October 1985 showed that 19 per cent believed Greenpeace vessels should be free to cruise off Moruroa and that 27 per cent were against France having nuclear bombs.[13] French supporters of a nuclear free and independent Pacific are appalled at the ignorance and parochialism of their countrymen. But the majority think otherwise. In his 1986 book, *Reflections on the Foreign Policy of France*, Mitterrand accused critics of picking on France over nuclear testing and said the sinking of the *Rainbow Warrior* did not 'change the substance of the debate'.[14] It was an act, he said, which had not engaged France morally. The French were not upset about *Rainbow Warrior*; therefore others could not use it as an argument against France's tests.

11

Crisis in ANZUS

In two years, from the election of the Lange Labour government in New Zealand in July 1984 to the US Secretary of State's announcement in June 1986 that America and New Zealand were parting company, the political landscape of the South Pacific changed markedly. New Zealand became a champion of the anti-nuclear cause in the region, opposed to both the USA and France on the issue. Australia led smaller countries of the South Pacific in fashioning a limited form of nuclear free zone. The French, their colonies and bombs, were resented by the people of the South Pacific as never before. And the Americans' security treaty with Australia and New Zealand collapsed, although its provisions continue to apply to Australia. Nuclear politics in the South Pacific assumed a new importance.

From the time David Lange became the Labour Prime Minister of New Zealand the Americans became gradually aware that an old ally, so trustworthy that it had been virtually forgotten, no longer wanted to do everything Washington asked. Lange came to office declaring that New Zealand would no longer permit nuclear-armed ships to come into its ports. In effect, he was denying port access to any vessel of the US Navy which as a matter of policy will neither confirm nor deny whether nuclear weapons are being carried. For six months the Americans thought that a little friendly pressure and perhaps an ambiguously phrased arrangement between Washington and Wellington would ensure that New Zealand changed its tune. Instead, the Lange government stuck by its policy.

Early in February 1985, New Zealand twice rejected American requests for port facilities for the USS *Buchanan*, a warship capable of carrying nuclear weapons. Suddenly the American media began saying that something called the ANZUS Treaty was now in danger of collapsing, and that this would be a bad thing for the USA. Most Americans had never heard of ANZUS. It turned out to be a security treaty between Australia, New Zealand and the USA, signed in San Francisco in 1951 and in force since 1952. The key provision of the treaty, in article IV, said: 'Each Party recognizes that an armed attack in the Pacific Area on any of the Parties would be dangerous to its own peace and safety and declares that it would act to meet the common danger in accordance with its constitutional processes.' The treaty was part of a broader military alliance with America's friends down under, with whom the Americans exchanged intelligence, conducted joint military exercises and co-operated generally in defence matters. From the American point of view, it kept the South Pacific safely out of harm's way and under Western strategic control. Why the New Zealanders should wish to place this happy arrangement in jeopardy was beyond the understanding of most observers in the USA. The price of accepting visits by an ally's warships seemed a small one for the protection received in return.

The State Department expressed the growing impatience of the Reagan Administration with New Zealand: 'We believe alliances require interaction of military forces and equitable burden sharing. Some Western countries have anti-nuclear movements which seek to diminish defence co-operation among allied States. We would hope that our response to New Zealand would signal that the course these movements advocate would not be cost-free in terms of security relationships with the US.' White House spokesman Larry Speakes said it was 'a matter of grave concern' that New Zealand had excluded the USS *Buchanan*.[1] Irritated, the USA withdrew from the ANZUS maritime exercise called 'Sea Eagle', due to be held in March 1985, and Australia announced its cancellation. The flow of American intelligence to New Zealand began to dry up.

Opinion polls showed that American disapproval failed

to change the New Zealanders' views about nuclear ship visits. In answer to the question 'Do you support or oppose visits to New Zealand ports by nuclear-armed warships?' 30 per cent were in favour, 59 per cent against and 11 per cent did not know in August 1985, compared with 30 per cent, 58 per cent and 12 per cent a year previously. Lange had the majority behind him. After all, in the elections which brought him to power, 64 per cent of voters supported parties in favour of banning nuclear ships.[2] Attempting to explain this attitude, the *New York Times* said it derived from New Zealand's defensiveness, pride and tradition of being 'a nation of reformers';[3] then there was the fact that their stand against the USA put the New Zealanders in the geopolitical spotlight as never before. As if to confirm that New Zealand now occupied centre-stage as an anti-nuclear nation, the French sank *Rainbow Warrior* there. Lange made the most of the affair. 'We are an enemy of the nuclear threat and we are an enemy of testing nuclear weapons in the South Pacific,' he said in September 1985. 'France puts spies into New Zealand. France lets bombs off in the Pacific. France puts its President in the Pacific to crow about it. It is not the New Zealand or the Pacific way of doing things ... '[4]

Lange was adamant that the USA would not force New Zealand to accept nuclear weapons. He said he would not back down because of American pressure: 'The old defence relationship which allowed nuclear weapons to be brought into New Zealand is at an end.'[5] And while Lange introduced a bill to formalise the ban on nuclear ship visits, the Americans hastened to find an experienced and senior career diplomat, Paul Cleveland, to become the new American Ambassador in Wellington. In confirmation hearings before the US Senate, Cleveland warned that any New Zealand legislation confirming the ship-visits policy would lead to the end of ANZUS. To drive the message home to the rebellious New Zealanders Washington refused to accept the visit of a delegation which was to explain the proposed legislation to the US State Department. Stephen Solarz, the New York Democrat who is Chairman of the Subcommittee on Asian and Pacific Affairs in the US House of Representatives, went to New Zealand early in 1986 with a smile on his face and talked about a 'separation' rather than a 'divorce' between the two countries. He said it had been possible in the past 'to square the circle'.[6] But Solarz was merely saying what had been said before: that, by adopting a face-saving formula in the law on ship visits, the conflict could be settled on American terms.

The US Navy is increasingly a nuclear navy. Two hundred and eighty-nine of the 342 major ships are capable of carrying nuclear weapons. But New Zealand ports are of little strategic importance to the Americans. Only 41 US Navy vessels visited New Zealand between 1976 and 1984. The Americans got tough with Lange not because New Zealand mattered militarily but in order to stop the rot from spreading. In the opinion of the USA Secretary of State, George Schultz, it 'would be a tragedy for freedom and Western values for the policy of New Zealand to spread'. No doubt he had in mind the encouragement which New Zealand has given to anti-nuclear lobbies in Australia, Japan and even European countries.

The potential effect in Australia was demonstrated at the Palm Sunday Peace Rally in Sydney in 1985, an event which drew as many as 170 000 people on to the streets and to the Domain afterwards. The crowd applauded the speech given by the New Zealand Labour MP, Helen Clark, and then heckled the peace message from the Australian government. At the back of the rally a huge banner read: 'New Zealand Leads the Way'. The US Consul General in Sydney, John Dorrance, an expert in South Pacific affairs, recognised the danger. In a paper called 'ANZUS: Misperceptions, Mythology and Reality', he described as a 'myth' the idea that ANZUS could be denuclearised and that Australia should follow New Zealand's lead. 'With words,' said the Consul, 'New Zealand assures its partners that it remains committed to ANZUS; by its deeds New Zealand has effectively curtailed its defense cooperation and operational role in ANZUS.'[7]

The last thing the Australian government wanted was an end to ANZUS. By staying friends with both Washington and Wellington, and by expanding defence co-operation with New Zealand, it tried to keep ANZUS in a state of cold storage from which it could be revived in the future. Australia remained firmly wedded to the American alliance. Yet even here, in the jewel of America's South Pacific crown, people were questioning the value of ANZUS as never before. They were asking whether it was more a risk than a benefit to ensure that the

Soviets trained missiles on Australia by giving them natural targets in the form of the American bases. Anti-nuclear sentiment was riding high and the government could no longer ignore it.

To begin with, the Americans had been delighted with Bob Hawke, the Labor Prime Minister elected in March 1983. When he went to Washington a few months later, he heaped praise on the American President, as many other Australian prime ministers have done in the past. Australia's review of the ANZUS Treaty in 1983 also pleased the USA. After careful consideration, Australia concluded that ANZUS was of such merit that no changes to the treaty could improve it. According to the Hawke government, the strategic interests of the USA and Australia coincided.

The embarrassment of the *Invincible* affair was also smoothed over as the Americans wished. Australia barred HMS *Invincible*, a British aircraft carrier almost certainly carrying nuclear weapons, from dry dock facilities in Sydney Harbour in December 1983. Australian Labor Party (ALP) policy forbids nuclear weapons on Australian soil, and the Minister for Defence applied the policy literally. But after a phone call from the Australian Foreign Minister, Bill Hayden, to George Shultz, and discussions between Australia, Britain and the USA, a new policy for dry docking quietly emerged early in 1984. Australia 'would not in any way endanger the safety of any allied or friendly ship in need of access to Australian facilities.'[8]

On the question of the American bases at North-West Cape, Pine Gap and Nurrungar, which Washington regards as vital links in its worldwide nuclear chain, Hawke proved equally accommodating. After obtaining clearance from the Americans who checked his speech beforehand, Hawke made a statement about the facilities in June 1984. He revealed nothing new and claimed that the facilities were 'not military bases'.[9] Australians were left to ponder just what North-West Cape, Pine Gap and Nurrungar were, and why these facilities were potential nuclear targets.

Reassuringly for America, the Hawke government linked arms control directly with the ANZUS alliance, claiming that other countries would listen to Australia only if it remained a staunch US ally. Hayden said that having the American bases on Australian soil somehow conferred 'moral standing' on Australian disarmament policies at the UN: 'We don't believe on the one hand that we can be credible in arguing the case for improved, more effective arms control measures, and on the other hand bailing out of all responsibility to maintain some sort of nuclear stability and restraint in the world.'[10] Yet even as Hayden tried to convince people that arms control was a major concern of the Labor government, peace groups sceptical of the government line were springing up all over Australia. The rot which America feared was spreading.

The 1984 Federal Election campaign in Australia showed that a sizeable minority of voters wanted American bases out of the country and an end to ANZUS. To many dissident Australians, New Zealand's one simple symbolic stroke in keeping out nuclear ships seemed to have done more for peace than all the elaborate arms control diplomacy of their own government; and the difference lay in the fact that New Zealand had dared to step outside the strict confines of ANZUS and risk American retaliation. Lange's ship-visits policy made Hayden look timid and ineffectual. A new political grouping suddenly emerged to fill the political void, the Nuclear Disarmament Party (NDP), and won a Western Australian seat in the Senate. The NDP won nine per cent of the Senate vote in New South Wales, 9.7 per cent in the Australian Capital Territory and 6.9 per cent in Victoria.[11] Disaffected members of the ALP, admirers of Lange rather than Hawke, broke ranks to vote in large numbers for the new party, some even helping the NDP on polling booths in defiance of ALP rules. Altogether, anti-nuclear parties willing to risk the ANZUS Treaty on the issue won almost 15 per cent of the Senate vote. When the Hawke government was re-elected, it came under pressure from within the Labor Party itself to take anti-nuclear sentiment in the country more seriously.

The first real victory of the anti-nuclear movement in Australia came early in 1985 when the Reagan Administration discovered that not even their good friend Hawke could deliver everything they wanted. A revolt within his own party forced the Prime Minister to withdraw his promise that Australia would provide logistical support for the testing of MX intercontinental ballistic missiles over the Pacific. The MX or 'missile experimental', has been more controversial in the USA than any other nuclear weapon since the beginning of the arms race in 1946. It is designed to carry ten nuclear bombs, each programmed to hit a different target. The initial flight test of the MX was delayed for six months by Congressional opposition, and finally took place between California and Kwajalein atoll in June 1983. Congress having voted funds for limited development of the new weapon, more MX tests followed. Meantime a select trio in Canberra, the Prime Minister and the Ministers for Defence and Foreign Affairs, had secretly assured the Reagan Administration that Australia would help the US military in a long-range test of the MX across the Pacific to a splash-down point in the ocean south-east of Tasmania.

But the secret was revealed just as Hawke left for an overseas trip in February 1985, and while he was away influential politicians from all factions of the ALP publicly criticised the government's decision. A strong Hawke supporter in Victoria, Alan Griffiths, attacked the MX and complained that the Cabinet had been by-passed. He spoke for the majority in the ALP. After all, the Hawke government had just campaigned for re-election on the promise that peace and disarmament occupied a 'pivotal place' in its foreign policy and that the ALP was the 'real disarmament party'; yet here it was, within a few months, offering Australian assistance in developing a deadly weapon over which even the Americans were sharply divided. As his party deserted him, Hawke had no option but to back down. When he reached Washington for talks with Schultz his sudden change of mind provoked accusations from American newspapers that Australia had reneged on a promise and had dealt a new blow to the ANZUS alliance.

Confronted with two separate ANZUS crises in the same week, officials in the Reagan Administration decided to distinguish clearly between Hawke and Lange. Hawke was a friend who would do all he could to protect American strategic interests in Australia, especially the bases; if the Americans were to complain about Hawke going back on his promise it would only undermine his position as Prime Minister and encourage anti-nuclear sentiment in his party; better therefore to say that the USA, of its own accord, had decided to test MX over the Pacific without Australian facilities. Lange, on the other hand, was obviously not as pro-American as he ought to be and would respond only to punishment; he needed to learn the lesson that New Zealand was not free to determine its foreign policy. The distinction was spelt out by a senior Defense official in Washington who said that the MX was a 'totally different question' from banning access to American ships.[12] In other words, Hawke did not threaten ANZUS but Lange did.

Lange's determination to pass legislation making New Zealand nuclear-free finally provoked a firm declaration from the Americans. Speaking in Manila in June 1986, the American Secretary of State said that New Zealand had withdrawn itself from the ANZUS alliance and that America's defence commitments to its former ally no longer applied. 'So we part company as friends,' said Schultz, 'but we part company.' The American position was confirmed six weeks later at the ANZUS council meeting in San Francisco, where the USA officially stated that it was 'suspending its security obligations to New Zealand under the ANZUS Treaty pending adequate corrective measures'.[13] The ANZUS Treaty now survives as an arrangement between Australia and the USA alone.

Since early 1985 military and intelligence co-operation between the USA and New Zealand has dried up. The USA withdrew invitations to New Zealand to participate in war games in America, South Korea and the Philippines; closed a New Zealand intelligence post at the Pacific Command Intelligence Centre in Hawaii; cancelled exchanges of military personnel; and blocked New Zealand access to information collected under the secret UKUSA Agreement, by which New Zealand co-operates with the USA, Britain, Australia and Canada in signals intelligence.[14] The US Secretary of the Navy, John Lehman, has urged the American government to go further and ban imports of New Zealand lamb, beef and other agricultural products. 'If foreign left-wing governments are able to assuage their left-wing, anti-nuclear radicals at the expense of the US Navy cost-free,' he said, then anti-nuclear policies were sure to spread.[15]

The American reaction to New Zealand undermined a fundamental assumption held by those Australians and New

Zealanders who favour the ANZUS alliance, namely, that by being always ready to assist the USA the small allies down under will win credit in Washington. The idea is that a history of helpfulness will be remembered by the Americans in time of need. But, says Fedor Mediansky, 'New Zealand's military contributions to the Western alliance during two world wars, Korea, Vietnam, and now the Sinai peacekeeping force, did not, in the end, generate sufficient credit for it in Washington to override the one important difference—even though the Lange government was locked into that difference by the democratic process and even though that difference does not impinge on the military posture of the USA in the South Pacific.'[16] The New Zealand Prime Minister is now under pressure from those within his own party who want to take the logic of the collapse of ANZUS a step further and declare New Zealand non-aligned.

Meantime Australia took the initiative in proposing a limited form of nuclear free zone in the South Pacific. The Americans have never shown enthusiasm for the idea.

'Unless carefully crafted,' a State Department expert said, 'a South Pacific Nuclear Free Zone could cripple the ability of US forces to exercise in the South Pacific with our ANZUS allies and to transit the South Pacific to Australia, New Zealand and the Indian Ocean in war or peace.'[17] Interviewed at the end of 1984, the former US Commander in Chief for the Pacific Admiral William J. Crowe hoped the zone would not have 'any deleterious effect'.[18] But the Admiral went on to indicate that America might not object to the right kind of nuclear free zone, in other words, one which left American strategic interests unaffected. It is precisely this kind of zone, designed to be acceptable to the USA, which Hawke first proposed to the South Pacific countries in 1983 and which was agreed upon in 1985. On the question of port access to nuclear vessels, for example, each country which signs the treaty will be free to act as it wishes. The treaty will not create an ocean full of defiant little New Zealands.

The Americans might not endorse even this moderate anti-nuclear arrangement. The principal political purpose of declaring a nuclear free zone is to further isolate France in the South Pacific and to bring an end to nuclear testing at Moruroa.

The zone is anti-French in conception. Yet for this very reason the Americans might refuse to sign the protocols to the treaty. The French nuclear force in Europe, rapidly growing, is seen by Washington as a valuable addition to the Western forces in NATO and a source of pressure on the Soviet Union. The Americans have come to like this independent, but in effect pro-American French defence policy, and they do not want to upset France. For European reasons the Americans are likely to back France in the South Pacific, whatever the South Pacific countries might say.

In any case, powerful forces in the Reagan Administration oppose nuclear free zones in principle, on the grounds that they will ultimately impede the passage of US warships through the oceans of the world. On a visit to Australia in 1986 the US Defense Secretary Caspar Weinberger said he thought a South Pacific nuclear free zone would 'advantage the aggressor power' and encourage the formation of such zones elsewhere.[19] He indicated displeasure with Australia over the issue.

The standing of both France and the USA has fallen in the South Pacific. The Australian Ambassador to the USA, Rawdon Dalrymple, offered an explanation for this decline in French and American reputations when he spoke to the Asia Society in Washington in September 1985. His speech, coolly received in the State Department, was a mark of the fear now held by the Hawke government that anti-nuclear sentiment in the South Pacific, fuelled by French testing, was undermining the US and Australian position in the area. The USA, said Dalrymple, was:

> ... seen as being less than helpful by the states of the South Pacific. And that is because the United States has tended, is seen anyway—to have tended, to side with France on the issue of nuclear testing in the South Pacific. It is considered in the region that the United States could, if it wanted to do so, exert strong influence on France to cease testing on Moruroa atoll. So far the United States has not only refrained from any such persuasion but has tended to give a good deal of credence to French arguments that the testing does no particular harm. Now I, and I am sure many other people in the South Pacific, understand very well the delicate nature of the relationship between the United States and the Western

defence alliance particularly in relation to the intricacies
of that alliance as it relates to the defence of Europe. But
the sentiment in the South Pacific is very much to the
effect that those concerns belong primarily in Europe. It
does not seem to people in the South Pacific that there is
any good reason why if the French want to have a so-
called *force de frappe* and want to test nuclear weapons
that they could not do so in areas closer to home.

It has been argued by the French that the particular
geological structure of Moruroa atoll is especially suitable
for nuclear weapons testing. But it is my understanding
that identical or anyway very similar geological structures
exist also in Corsica and in the Jura. But of course on
Moruroa atoll there are no French voters. There are,
however, (not on the atoll of course, but in the region) all
the inhabitants of the South Pacific who look to this
testing and feel that it is grossly unjust that a country
from the other side of the world should use their region
for this essentially and intrinsically dangerous purpose.
Whether the effects of radiation and so on are in fact
minimal, is not in their minds the primary issue.

Continued French testing at Moruroa, said Dalrymple, was
'absolutely certain to prejudice the South Pacific people against
the West, against that is to say United States and Australian
interests in a way that will quite possibly prove very costly'.
And that same French testing, he added, had been 'a major
influence in the formation of the climate of opinion in New
Zealand which is now causing such anxiety to both the United
States and the Australian Governments in relation to the
future of ANZUS'. The Australian Ambassador's message to
the Americans was a simple one: for the sake of their own
interests in the South Pacific and in order to prevent the
Soviet Union from winning friends among the Island peoples,
the USA should lean on the French to stop Pacific tests.[20]

In promoting a moderate nuclear free zone the Hawke
government is trying to channel anti-nuclear sentiment in the
South Pacific away from radical measures of the kind taken by
New Zealand. The zone would be safe, even if not ideal, for
the USA. And in urging the USA to use its influence to bring
French nuclear explosions in the Pacific to an end, Australia
seeks to remove a powerful symbol for the anti-nuclear movements in the region. As New Zealand shows, opposition to

nuclear weapons logically becomes opposition to ANZUS, which is a nuclear alliance.

Within Australia the Hawke government seeks similar ends. It is a short step from 'I am against nuclear weapons' to 'I am against ANZUS, which makes Australia a nuclear target'. Concious of this, the government is attempting to redirect and contain the anti-nuclear energies of the peace movement before they threaten the American alliance. It constantly stresses its dedication to the cause of peace and disarmament, and its record on arms control is certainly more impressive than that of the previous, conservative government. Labor under Hawke has appointed Australia's first Ambassador for Disarmament; it has funded a Peace Research Institute and set up a peace and disarmament branch of the Department of Foreign Affairs; at the Conference on Disarmament in Geneva it has pushed hard, though with no success so far, for a comprehensive nuclear test ban treaty; it has ratified the Inhumane Weapons Convention and the Environmental Modification Convention, which is designed to prevent the development of new military techniques such as the artificial creation of earthquakes, changes in weather or interference with the ozone layer; it contributes in a minor way to the disarmament activities of the UN and supported the International Year of Peace in 1986; and it has proposed and then successfully negotiated the nuclear free zone treaty. None of these things should be disparaged by those who seek to free Australia from the nuclear web, and not all of them have been welcomed in Washington, especially Australia's enthusiasm for a comprehensive test ban treaty.

Yet at the same time Australia has been careful not to take peace initiatives to the point of threatening the American alliance. On fundamentals of defence policy the present Australian Labor government is hard to distinguish from the previous conservative government under Malcolm Fraser. The policy on ship-visits, for example, has been inherited from Fraser almost without change: nuclear-armed or nuclear-powered vessels are welcome to come to Australian ports and the government does not ask Australia's allies to confirm or deny whether their ships are carrying nuclear weapons. Australia under Labor expressed its understanding of the NATO decision to deploy Pershing II and cruise missiles in Western

Europe; it has repeatedly defended the presence of the American bases on the grounds that they contribute to something called 'stable deterrence'; it gives its full support to Australia's active involvement in the nuclear fuel cycle through the export of uranium, even to France; and it appears to have brought pressure to bear on the New Zealand government to abandon its ship-visits policy in the interests of the ANZUS alliance. Except for the revolt in the ALP, the Hawke government would have helped the Americans test the MX missiles. The Foreign Minister Hayden is more frank than his conservative predecessors about the dangers to Australia of hosting American bases, which he says would be targets of 'high priority' in a nuclear war,[21] and he has talked of using the bases as bargaining counters with the Americans: to make Washington take arms control more seriously, for example, or to dissuade the Americans from undercutting Australian wheat sales to the Soviet Union. But the end result for Australia is the same: Australia supports a nuclear alliance, identifies itself with America's worldwide ambitions and is prepared to see nuclear weapons used on its behalf.

12

Becoming nuclear free

War will remain for as long as the world consists of sovereign states, each arming against its enemies; and nuclear war will remain a possibility for as long as sovereign states possess nuclear weapons. However, a general nuclear war would be unlike any previous war. Not only would it bring the lives of hundreds of millions of people to an end; it would close the curtain on human history itself. The growing appreciation of this fact by the peoples of the Pacific, together with their experience of nuclear testing, has produced a nuclear phobia in the region. A simple idea—however difficult it might be to execute—is now on the political agenda of numerous popular organisations in the Pacific and is regarded seriously by most independent countries south of the equator. That idea is to make the Pacific nuclear free.

The origin of the movement for a nuclear free and independent Pacific can be traced to the ATOM committee (Against Tests on Moruroa) which was formed in Fiji in 1970 to protest against French testing. It consisted of individuals from the Pacific Theological College, the University of South Pacific and the Fiji YWCA. Backed by the Pacific Conference of Churches, the ATOM committee helped to organise the first conference for a nuclear free Pacific, held in Fiji in 1975.[1] More conferences followed, each time embracing wider political constituencies: on the Micronesian island of Pohnpei in 1978, in Hawaii in 1980 and in the independent South Pacific state of Vanuatu in 1983. The nuclear free movement initiated by the churches now includes a wide variety of organisations across the Pacific as well as in Japan, the Philippines, the

133

USA, Canada, Australia and New Zealand. Trade unions, private aid organisations, environmentalists, disarmament lobbies, women's collectives and Christian groups co-operate in a loosely organised network, exchanging information and visits, holding conferences and publicising the concept of a nuclear free Pacific.

Compared with the prodigious wealth and gargantuan military might of the American, Soviet and French nuclear forces in the Pacific, this movement is puny indeed, its combined resources amounting to a tiny fraction of the cost of a single nuclear weapon. Critics say the movement demands such a radical change in the security relationships of Pacific countries that it is doomed to irrelevance. But this is to misunderstand the power and status of the nuclear free idea in the Pacific Islands. Over a period of 10 years, and especially since the early 1980s when public alarm about the arms race revived, the objective of freeing the Pacific Islands from all things nuclear has been legitimised; and while the movement's achievements fall far short of radical change, it has enjoyed some successes. Its lobbying has helped to dissuade the Japanese, so far, from dumping radioactive waste in the deep ocean trenches off the Northern Mariana Islands in the north Pacific; and because of the movement's complaints, the military forces of Australia and Japan no longer bombard the island of Kaho'olawe during annual exercises with the Americans, in deference to the cultural significance of the island to native Hawaiians. Who would have predicted in 1980 that within six years the independent countries of the South Pacific would be seeking to establish a nuclear free zone? Or that the ANZUS Treaty would have been in abeyance because the New Zealanders refused to be defended by nuclear weapons? Or that the forces in favour of the nuclear free constitution in Belau would have resisted the USA for so long?

Organised Christianity has played a significant part in pressing for a nuclear free and independent Pacific. The Pacific Conference of Churches, which embraces the Catholic and all the mainstream Protestant churches of the South Pacific, stands for thorough denuclearisation of the region. It opposes not only French testing and the dumping of nuclear wastes but also the passage of nuclear submarines and ships. With their village networks and strong followings in what is one of the most Christianised parts of the globe, the churches mobilise opinion more effectively than any other institution. They also have links to the outside world. A World Council of Churches team was in the Marshall Islands in 1982 during *Operation Homecoming* when people were reoccupying the islands of the atoll and disrupting the American missile testing program. A second World Council of Churches delegation, which included a nuclear physicist, went to the Marshall Islands in 1983 and published a report criticising US policy. The delegation said the 'serious, unique health problems' of the Marshallese as a consequence of US testing demanded a comprehensive solution involving care for the whole population. A minor scandal erupted when a senior official in the Reagan Administration got his facts wrong and accused the World Council of Churches of disseminating propaganda 'behind the facade of a religious undertaking'. What particularly worried him was the fact that criticism of the USA would be carried by the world wide distribution system of the World Council of Churches to millions of people. The World Council responded by saying that it made no apology 'for taking the side of the victims of oppression'.[2]

The Pacific Trade Union Forum, a joint organisation of trade unions in the South Pacific, also takes a nuclear free stance; and since 1984 a 'Free Trade Union Institute' in Fiji, generously funded from American sources, has been trying to counter the influence of nuclear free unions with a program of conferences, trips and money for Pacific Islanders. In the view of the Institute, the ability of Island union leaders 'to draw distinctions between the Soviet bloc and the democratic nations of the world is sometimes clouded, especially when emotional issues such as colonialism, nuclear testing and economic protection zones are introduced into discussion'.[3] The USA wants to bring American-style unionism to the Islands.

A conference which might earn a few lines on the back page of the newspaper if it were held in the USA or Australia is a major event in a small Island state. Such was the case with the nuclear free and independent Pacific conference in Port Vila, Vanuatu, in 1983. It was opened by the Deputy Prime Minister, Sethy Regenvanu, and the keynote speech was given by Barak Sope, Secretary-General of the ruling Vanuaaku party. Sope stressed the central contention of the movement: that the Pacific Islands will not be nuclear free until they are truly independent, and that the nuclear history of the Pacific arises from its lack of independence. If the people of the Marshall Islands had not been under the political control of a foreign power in the 1940s and 1950s, testing would probably not have taken place there; if French Polynesia had not been a colony in the 1960s, France would have had to test elsewhere; an independent New Caledonia of the kind wanted by most of the Melanesian population would follow the example of its neighbour Vanuatu and keep nuclear vessels out of its ports, just as an independent Belau would retain its nuclear free constitution. Given the choice, Pacific Islanders would prefer not to have their ocean made a nuclear playground for foreigners to make explosions and fire missiles. But choice is limited for all Islanders and closed off completely for those who still live in colonies. Barak Sope said, 'The people of Tahiti have no choice ... whether a nuclear bomb is tested in their country or not. It is the French government who makes the choice. The Republic of Vanuatu is becoming a nuclear free state, because it is the ni-Vanuatu [people of Vanuatu] who have decided on this—not the British or the French who were the former colonial powers.'[4]

The conference in Vanuatu adopted a 'People's Charter for a Nuclear Free and Independent Pacific'. 'Our environment,' says the charter, 'continues to be despoiled by foreign powers developing nuclear weapons for a strategy of warfare that has no winners, no liberators and imperils the survival of all humankind.' Military bases and testing facilities might bring employment to Pacific Islanders, 'but the price is destruction of our customs, our way of life, the pollution of our crystal clear waters and brings the ever present threat of disaster by radioactive poisoning into the every day lives of the peoples'.[5] The nuclear free zone envisaged in the charter would embrace Micronesia, Australia, the Philippines, Japan and Hawaii and would ban nuclear weapons even aboard ships. The anti-nuclear activists called upon Pacific governments to ban French warships from their ports until testing stops at Moruroa. They placed themselves on the side of the Kanaks in the independence struggle in New Caledonia; opposed the Indonesian government's policy of transmigration in Irian Jaya; denounced the presence of US military bases in the Philippines; endorsed a protest against the dumping of nuclear waste in the Pacific; condemned the use of Kwajalein atoll for the testing of the MX and other missiles; called for an end to the mining of uranium; and restated their support for Belau's nuclear free constitution. In other words, they stated the maximal claim for a nuclear free Pacific. Such a claim has no prospect of being implemented immediately. Yet at the same time it has become part of the world of ideas which influences the politicians of the region, especially those of the South Pacific Islands.

What happens to the aspiration for a nuclear free zone in the Pacific when it is translated into practical politics? The answer may be found in the South Pacific Nuclear Free Zone Treaty, adopted at a meeting of regional states in 1985.

The idea of nuclear free zones was prompted by the Antarctic Treaty of 1959. The Treaty showed that an entire continent, admittedly uninhabited, could be demilitarised and denuclearised. There was talk in the Australian Labor Party of such a zone for the Pacific in the early 1960s, and a petition to the New Zealand government in 1964 sought the declaration of a nuclear free southern hemisphere, but it was the 1967 Treaty for the Prohibition of Nuclear Weapons in Latin America, or Treaty of Tlatelolco, which provided a model to follow. The New Zealand Labour Government of 1972–75 then became the first in the region to make a serious proposal, supported by the South Pacific Forum at its 1975 meeting. Having backed New Zealand at the Forum, however, the Australian Labor government under Gough Whitlam began to have misgivings, prompted by the anxieties being expressed in Washington.

Whitlam told the New Zealand Prime Minister Wallace Rowling, that a nuclear free zone in the Pacific would 'disadvantage US strategic interests and its security arrangements in the South Pacific' and 'pose problems for ANZUS'. Because of Australian and American opposition, based on the fear that the zone might prevent visits by nuclear vessels, the New Zealand proposal was already running into the sands when the two Labor governments were defeated at the end of 1975. It was then quietly buried for eight years until Hawke presented his own version to the Forum in Canberra in August

1983. In both cases political leaders of the South Pacific favoured a nuclear free treaty because they felt affronted by continued French testing at Moruroa. The French, not the Americans, were the target.[6]

The South Pacific Forum, formed in 1971, brings together 13 independent or self-governing countries. Australia and New Zealand, because of their investments in the Islands, aid programs and expertise, dominate the Forum on crucial issues. Of the Island states, Papua New Guinea (population over three million) and Fiji (population 650 000) are the biggest. After that come the micro-states, none with more than 300 000 people and most with considerably fewer: Solomon Islands, Vanuatu, Tonga, Western Samoa, Kiribati, Tuvalu, Nauru, the Cook Islands and Niue. The remaining islands of the South Pacific are all French, British or American territories and therefore ineligible to join the Forum, although one territory under the Americans, the Federated States of Micronesia, is permitted to observe Forum meetings. Australia is the big fish in this particular pond and it got the kind of nuclear free zone it wanted. What mattered above all for the Hawke government was that the zone should not offend the Americans or endanger ANZUS, and at the 1984 meeting of the Forum in the tiny country of Tuvalu (population 8800) South Pacific countries declared that, in any proposed zone, they would keep their 'unqualified sovereign rights to decide for themselves . . . their security arrangements, and such questions as the access to their ports and airfields by vessels and aircraft of other countries'.[7]

The South Pacific Nuclear Free Zone Treaty, adopted by the Forum at its meeting in Rarotonga on 6 August 1985, was signed on the same day by Australia, New Zealand, Fiji, Cook Islands, Kiribati, Niue, Tuvalu and Western Samoa. Papua New Guinea signed on 16 September. In many ways the treaty simply puts a legal stamp on the existing nuclear situation in the South Pacific. None of the Forum countries possesses or wishes to acquire its own nuclear weapons. Australia, New Zealand, Papua New Guinea, Fiji, Tonga, Tuvalu, Western Samoa and Kiribati have all signed the Nuclear Non-Proliferation Treaty of 1968, binding them not to have their own nuclear weapons, and Vanuatu, the most radical country on this issue,

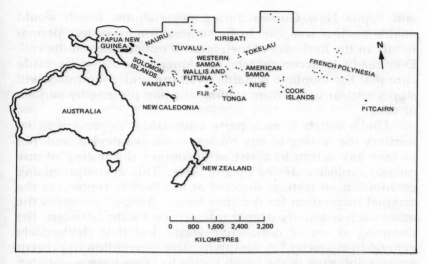

Area of the South Pacific Nuclear Free Zone. Of the thirteen South Pacific Forum countries, ten have so far signed the zone treaty: Australia, New Zealand, Papua New Guinea, Fiji, Western Samoa, Kiribati, Tuvalu, Niue, Cook Islands and Nauru. Three have not signed: Vanuatu, Solomon Islands and Tonga. The nuclear weapons states have been invited by the Forum to sign the protocols to the treaty.

declared itself nuclear free in 1982. So article 3 of the nuclear free zone treaty states what is already the case: each country promises 'not to manufacture or otherwise acquire, possess or have control over any nuclear explosive device by any means anywhere inside or outside the South Pacific Nuclear Free Zone'.

More significant is article 5, which bans the stationing of nuclear weapons, a provision which goes beyond the Non-Proliferation Treaty. This ban closes off the options of the superpowers in the future. Suppose, for example, that the USA has to withdraw from its huge military bases at Subic Bay and Clark Airfield in the Philippines. For as long as Australia adheres to the nuclear free zone treaty, the Americans would be barred from moving those bases to Australian soil. But there exists a loophole in the treaty, recognised by Vanuatu and Papua New Guinea during negotiations, which would enable nuclear weapons to be stationed more or less permanently in the harbours of the region if not actually on the soil. Ever ready to accommodate the Americans, Australia made sure that the loophole remains. Nothing under the treaty will stop a nuclear vessel from staying at a port for lengthy periods of time.

Under article 6, each party undertakes 'to prevent in its territory the testing of any nuclear explosive device' and 'not to take any action to assist or encourage the testing of any nuclear explosive device by any State.' This uncompromising prohibition on testing, directed at the French, represents the original inspiration for the zone treaty. Article 7 concerns the other nuclear activity deeply resented by Pacific Islanders, the dumping at sea of radioactive waste, but it is deliberately general in character.[8] A comprehensive convention to prevent nuclear dumping in the South Pacific has now been negotiated by a separate regional organisation, blessed with the bureaucratic name of the South Pacific Regional Environment Program.

The nuclear free zone is a distinctly limited arms control measure. The treaty will not stop ships, submarines and aircraft from carrying nuclear weapons through the South Pacific, nor will it prevent the testing of missiles in the region by the USA, the Soviet Union and China. The export of uranium from Australia is unaffected, and so are those vital links in the American nuclear chain, the US bases at North-West Cape, Pine Gap and Nurrungar, which will continue to fulfil their functions of command, control, communication and intelligence.

Even if France, China, the Soviet Union, the UK and the USA were to agree to everything in the treaty by the diplomatic action of signing its protocols, the nuclear presence in the South Pacific could still increase considerably: French testing would stop, but more French, Soviet and American submarines could traverse the region at will; more Chinese and American missiles could be tested; the nuclear firepower on board US vessels in Australian ports could grow unchecked; and the American bases could be used to order the firing of submarine-launched ballistic missiles. If they accepted the treaty, the nuclear weapons powers would promise not to fire nuclear missiles *against* countries in the zone, but the treaty offers no equivalent undertaking that such firing will not occur *from* countries in the zone, or to be precise, from their territorial waters. Since the Soviet invasion of Afghanistan in 1979, Soviet and American war planners have encouraged more aggressive surveillance and shadowing exercises by their nuclear navies in the north Pacific, as both sides practise for a possible war in the sea of Japan or off the Kamchatka Peninsula near the major Soviet base at Petropavlovsk. The Soviets and the Americans are arming for war in the Pacific; or, as the language of the military has it, the superpowers are engaged in upgrading their theatre nuclear postures. While the Soviet Union and the USA are at present unlikely to extend this naval competition south of the equator, they could do so without infringing the provisions of the South Pacific Nuclear Free Zone Treaty.[9]

The Treaty is a start, nothing more. And the very existence of something called a 'nuclear free zone' creates the false impression of considerable progress towards denuclearisation of the South Pacific. The Hawke government tells the Australian public that the zone means a lot, and at the same time hastens to reassure the Americans that it means little. It shares Washington's fears of a true nuclear free zone. As the former American Ambassador to Fiji, William Bodde, said in 1982: 'Should the South Pacific governments embrace a nuclear-free zone proposal, it would give us serious problems. Their position on dumping and on testing do not create any serious problems for the United States at this time since we neither dump nor test in the South Pacific. So it is the total ban on all things nuclear that represents the problem since some of the proposals envisage not only a ban on nuclear ships and submarines but also on planes with nuclear devices flying over the Pacific. That is just not acceptable to us strategically, and I think should be unacceptable to the Island Governments.'[10]

For some years Fiji was the Island state which most worried the Americans. It pressed for a nuclear free zone at the UN and in 1982 it barred nuclear powered or armed vessels from Fijian ports, saying that a refusal to confirm or deny the presence of nuclear weapons on board would be interpreted as an admission that they were being carried. Since 1983, however, the Americans have been assiduously wooing the Fiji government. The ship visits ban was dropped in that year, a decision which earned the Fiji Prime Minister Ratu Sir Kamisese Mara an accolade from President Reagan for having shown 'a high degree of political courage'.[11] When Ratu Mara went to the White House in November 1984 at the personal invitation of Reagan, he was the first South Pacific head of state to do so. He was then whisked off to New York to be made 'Pacific Man of the Year' by a supposedly independent organisation called the Foundation for the Peoples of the South Pacific; and just to make sure that Mara remained their friend, the Americans promised $300 000 for the Royal Fiji Military Forces. Mara makes frequent trips to the US Pacific military headquarters in Hawaii. The US objective in Fiji is to build up a safe ally among the Island states, now that New Zealand is seen as unreliable. Giving testimony to a US Congressional committee in 1986, a Reagan Administration official described Fiji as 'one of our staunchest supporters in the region . . . It has opened its ports to our warships at a time when powerful political forces in the region opposed such a move . . .'[12] The small Fiji Anti-Nuclear Group and the newly-formed Fiji Labour Party give expression to a wider disquiet in the country about the government's present foreign policy. When the 6900-tonne US nuclear-attack submarine *Portsmouth* paid a visit to Suva in January 1986 the Fiji government, afraid of popular opinion, did not announce the visit in advance, nor did the police permit a march of protest through the streets of the capital.[13]

By 1987 ten of the thirteen Forum countries had signed the nuclear free treaty and eight had ratified it. Vanuatu had announced that it would not sign because the treaty provisions were too weak. The Vanuatu Prime Minister Walter Lini said the treaty, being partial rather than comprehensive, would not stop the Russians, French and Americans from doing as they pleased in the region, and he predicted that people in the South Pacific would continue to want a truly nuclear free zone. At the 1986 meeting of the Forum in Fiji, Father Lini called for a treaty which would ban visits by nuclear ships and prevent the export of uranium from the region. But Lini and his allies in countries such as Solomon Islands remained isolated. Far from strengthening the treaty, the Forum further weakened it by inserting a clause which would allow any nuclear weapons state to withdraw from the treaty at short notice. Australia hoped that the treaty would now be inoffensive enough to attract the signatures of the USA and Britain. At the same time the Australian Labor government reversed party policy by lifting its ban on uranium sales to France. The ALP platform says that no such sales will occur 'until France ceases testing nuclear weapons in the South Pacific region', but the government claimed that, in harsh economic times, it could no longer afford to pay millions of dollars to the exporting company Queensland Mines.[14] The decision made many people question the seriousness of Australia's commitment to the nuclear free zone.

The paradox of our age is that nuclear weapons, which are supposed to uphold and preserve national security, succeed in achieving the opposite. We are far more threatened than protected by the bomb. It is not a weapon of defence, but a weapon of annihilation. Admiral Noel Gaylor, Commander in Chief of US Forces in the Pacific from 1972 to 1976, has said: 'When we built the atomic weapon, we built the one thing that could put the United States at risk.' Then when the Russians discovered the secret, 'We raised the ante by a factor of a thousand, and invented the hydrogen bomb. In consequence, defense, which had been made extraordinarily difficult by the arrival of the atomic bomb, now became impossible with the advent of the H—bomb, and so it remains.'[15] There followed a nuclear arms race between the Soviets and the Americans, from bombers to missiles to submarines to multiple warheads to cruise missiles and now, probably, to laser weapons in space, each step in that race diminishing rather than increasing the security of the superpowers.

Just as nuclear weapons put the superpowers at risk, so they endanger the rest of the world, including the superpower allies. The allies can find no way of making the superpowers take arms control seriously. The New Zealand Labour MP Helen Clark argues that nuclear alliances such as ANZUS are so lopsided in favour of the nuclear powers that they are hardly alliances at all: the role of the non-nuclear members, such as Australia and New Zealand, is simply to fit in with the plans of the major partner and to become unquestioning auxiliaries, marching lockstep into oblivion behind the leader.[16] In introducing a bill to make New Zealand a nuclear free zone, the Lange government has decided New Zealanders are safer without the defence provided by nuclear weapons. By declaring its independence on the nuclear issue New Zealand wishes to stop contributing to the competitive insecurity of the nuclear arms race.

Self-interest might also drive Australia to become nuclear free. The Nurrungar early warning facility was described in a recent US study as the 'single most important strategic base in the Pacific'.[17] According to Australia's Foreign Minister: 'The nuclear targetting doctrines of the great powers make it clear that the control, communications and intelligence functions of the kind performed by the joint US-Australian facilities we have in our country could be targets as prime as any in the world.'[18] In a war between the superpowers Australia would be hit, parts of the country obliterated and the rest contaminated by radioactive fallout. Yet what, apart from a pat on the back from Washington, does Australia get in return for standing exposed to the missiles? The official answer stresses access to Western intelligence, the advantages of military co-operation with the USA and the probability, no more, that the Americans would assist Australia in the event of an attack. In the case of Australia's most likely military encounter—hostilities with Indonesia along the border between west and east New Guinea —who is to say that the Americans would not support their allies the Indonesians rather than their allies the Australians? At the very least the USA might simply stand aside from the conflict.

Even as a conventional defence arrangement, the Australian-American alliance is of uncertain value to the junior partner; as a nuclear alliance it is opposed to Australia's national interest. The Australian government justifies the presence of American bases on its soil by saying that they contribute to 'stable deterrence' by giving the USA early warning of a Soviet nuclear attack. But 'stable deterrence' is a figment of the imagination; it does not exist. If it existed there would be

evidence of stability in superpower relations. Instead the superpowers engage in an unstable arms race, both espousing war-
fighting doctrines, both making plans to use nuclear weapons.
The Americans talk about being the first to use nuclear weapons
in a conventional conflict and about 'winning' a protracted
nuclear war. The Soviets do not rule out a massive first strike
in defence of their homeland. With the American bases removed and a national nuclear free zone declared, Australia
would be a safer place to live.

In Australia, as in the Pacific Islands, the nuclear issue is
a question of independence. Constitutionally independent
since the beginning of the century, Australia has always looked
overseas for a Great Protector in matters of defence: Britain
until 1942, America since then. The attitude, essentially a
colonial one, has not changed. Australians seek to win the
favour of the Great Protector by being always ready to assist,
whether at Gallipoli in 1915 or Korea in the 1950s or Vietnam
in the 1960s or North West Cape, Pine Gap and Nurrungar in
the 1980s. The hope is that the Great Protector, flattered by
these attentions, will remember Australia in times of need.
But more and more Australians now say that nothing is to be
gained by trying to win credit in one of the superpower
capitals and everything is to be lost, because minor allies are
nothing more than convenient places for putting nuclear installations. There is talk of a self-defence policy which would
send no aggressive signals to the rest of the world. Formal
treaties do not determine what countries do anyway. Despite
ANZUS, the USA supported Indonesia against Australia over
the question of who was to have west New Guinea in the
early 1960s. Without ANZUS, the USA would still come to
Australia's aid if the Americans thought that to do so was in
their national interest.

The American historian and former diplomat George F.
Kennan, who once helped to construct America's post-war
policy of containing Communism, now concludes that there is
no issue at stake between the USA and the Soviet Union, 'no
hope, no fear, nothing to which we aspire, nothing we would
like to avoid—which could conceivably be worth a nuclear
war'.[19] In the same way Australia, New Zealand and the Pacific

Island states have no issue in their relations with other countries which could conceivably be worth the use of nuclear weapons on their behalf.

The history of the South Pacific since 1946 suggests that, for as long as the region stays in the nuclear web of the USA and France, the safety of its people will be endangered.

13

Epilogue

Few people expect to survive nuclear war, and few believe that nuclear war could be limited once it began. If human populations still existed after a general nuclear conflict they would live in an unprecedentedly hostile environment, which poisoned them even as it sustained them. The idea that there could be historians in such a radioactive world, and that they could sit calmly at their wordprocessors assessing the past, is fanciful. No academic debate about the causes of World War III will ever occur. In order to understand the nuclear threat in the Pacific, however, we might profitably suspend disbelief for a moment and read from the pages of an imaginary history of the origins of the Third World War:

The question which has puzzled us of the Remnant, the survivors of the Catastrophe, is why the war started in the Pacific rather than Europe or the Middle East. All nuclear powers except China had long given strategic priority to the European theatre and competed there for military superiority. Talks between the superpowers, such as those between Reagan and Gorbachev in 1985, concentrated on what they saw as the region of greatest danger, Europe; and the possibility of a nuclear war developing from a Middle East conflict in which the USA backed Israel and the Soviet Union backed Syria had been feared universally. Yet the first shots fired at each other by Soviet and American forces since the 1920s came in the western Pacific, when ships of the Soviet Pacific Fleet did battle with those of the American Seventh Fleet near the Philippines. The war began as a naval confrontation.

The deeper causes of the war are clear. In the first place, both superpowers added numerous nuclear weapons to their arsenals during the 1980s. On the Soviet side Yankee-class submarines carrying SS−N−6 ballistic missiles; Delta-class submarines with SS−N−8s; surface and submarine-launched nuclear cruise missiles; land-based SS−20s on mobile launchers and long-range Backfire bombers. On the American side Ohio submarines carrying 192 nuclear bombs each on Trident missiles; thousands of sea-launched Tomahawk cruise missiles; 12 aircraft carriers with a total of more than a thousand fighter-interceptor, ground-attack and anti-submarine aircraft and new carrier battle groups. These were the chips that were played in the game of response and counter-response. And their effect, as we now know, was to narrow the non-nuclear options in the event of conflict.

In explaining why Pacific military forces were so rapidly nuclearised in the decade before the war we must remember the economic burden placed upon the superpowers by the need to keep great numbers of men and women under arms: 5 300 000 in the Soviet Union and 2 150 000 in the USA. Extraordinarily expensive though they were, nuclear weapons were seen as cheaper than huge conventional forces. Competition between different sectors of the armed forces also encouraged nuclearisation. Ever since the 1950s the US Navy, Army and Air Force had competed for nuclear attack roles in America's Pacific war plans. The Navy, whose Seventh Fleet had by 1990 become a massive force for the fighting of tactical nuclear war, was the most successful in this interservice rivalry and aspired to an independent voice in deciding what happened within its area of command. The Commander in Chief Pacific, based in Honolulu, is widely believed to have ignored the orders of the President soon after the war began. The Soviet Pacific Fleet, largest of the four Soviet naval fleets, appears to have outmanoeuvred the Far Eastern Military District Air Force in a similar contest for nuclear supremacy. Adding to these factors, of course, was the general deterioration of east-west relations during the 1980s, arrested briefly in the middle of Reagan's second term as President only to intensify thereafter in the deadlock over the Americans' Star Wars initiative.

The arms race in the Pacific was part of a wider phenomenon, though more dangerous than elsewhere because less widely recognised. The arms race in cruise missiles, for example, went almost unnoticed in many countries of the Pacific and the Far East, yet it contributed substantially to tension between the superpowers. Cruise missiles were pilotless jet aircraft capable of reaching targets with extreme accuracy and of flying low over terrain in order to escape detection by radar. Their introduction into western Europe in the early 1980s had caused a political storm. Peace movements, revitalised by the fear that the USA and the Soviet Union would make Europe their nuclear battlefield, tried to block deployment of the weapons. Land-based and mobile, the missiles were highly visible objects of protest by peace activists at sites such as Greenham Common in England; and their deployment in five countries rather than West Germany alone, a policy which was intended by NATO to show the Russians that the western Europeans stood united, had the effect of encouraging the spread of peace movements across the continent. But the coming of far more cruise missiles to the Pacific met with little opposition. Carried on board surface vessels and submarines, the sea-launched missiles were far less visible. By the time war broke out, the Americans had equipped their cruisers, submarines, destroyers and battleships with more than 3000 Tomahawk cruise missiles out of the 4068 originally planned, and of these, 483 were the T−LAM (N)BGM−109A version, which was tipped with a nuclear warhead 15 times more powerful than the Hiroshima bomb. The Soviet equivalent, known as the SS−NX−21, was also placed in large numbers on ships and submarines of the Soviet Pacific Fleet.

Both superpowers were responsible for the nuclear arms race, which derived its dynamic from the fact that each sought a balance of power decisively in its favour. The Russians indicated a major shift in strategic priorities in 1979 when they created a new headquarters for the Far Eastern Theatre of Military Operations at Chita near Manchuria, 400 kilometres east of Lake Baikal. From here commands went to the Central Asian, Siberian, Transbaikal and Far Eastern Military Districts as well as forces in Mongolia. It was in 1979, too, that the Russians began to establish an important military presence in Vietnam, by moving into the former American facilities at Da Nang and Cam Ranh. Vietnam gave the Soviet Union valuable access to the South China Sea and the Pacific without the problems of winter ice encountered by the Soviet Pacific Fleet north of China.

From the airfields at Cam Ranh Soviet MiG−23 Flogger interceptors provided fighter escort for the Navy; TU−95 Bear D reconnaissance and TU−142 Bear F anti-submarine warfare aircraft kept a constant watch on the movements of American and allied forces; TU−16 and occasionally Backfire long-range bombers came and went, inspiring fear in Southeast Asian countries that the Russians were intent on aggression. And from Cam Ranh Bay about 30 Soviet naval vessels, including submarines, undertook regular sorties into the South China Sea. Although naval forces in Vietnam were small beside those stationed at Vladivostok and Sovetskaya Gavan in the Sea of Japan and Petropavlovsk on the Kamchatka Peninsula, they became valuable justification for the US Navy in its ambitions to become a giant 600-ship navy with 15 carrier battle groups. Together, the growth in Soviet naval power in the western Pacific and the Iranian hostage crisis of 1979 were the starting points of massive naval expansion by the USA in the 1980s. They provided the arguments which convinced the American public that the Pacific had to remain an American lake at all costs.

Even before America's decision to give the Pacific greater prominence in its global military planning, half the US Navy was there, operating from naval bases at Midway; Yokosuka, Japan; Apra Harbor, Guam; and Subic Bay in the Philippines. At Subic, one of the biggest bases outside the USA, 36 000 Filipinos worked alongside 6000 US Navy personnel and the inhabitants of the entire city of Olongapo could thank the USA for their livelihoods. US bases and installations dotted the region: 119 of them in Japan and Okinawa alone, and more in South Korea, the island of Diego Garcia in the Indian Ocean, Micronesia, Hawaii and Australia. The most important facilities in Japan were Yokota Air Base, home to the USAF Fifth Air Force, Yokosuka naval base, headquarters for US

Naval Forces Japan, and the intelligence station at Misawa which swept the Sea of Japan, the Sea of Okhotsk and the Soviet Far East for information about Soviet military activity. Among numerous bases in South Korea, where the US Army kept some 30 000 troops, was Kunsan Air Base, the site of a nuclear weapons storage depot. The base at Diego Garcia was developed in the 1980s to support America's Rapid Deployment Force for use in protecting US interests in South Asia and the Persian Gulf. It could anchor an entire carrier task force in its atoll lagoon. To the east, Hawaii, America's state in the Pacific, was headquarters for the Commander in Chief Pacific, whose task was to co-ordinate virtually all US military operations in the region.

Many people in the West felt comforted by the fact that, during the 1980s, America was 'maintaining a credible military presence' in the Pacific and 'enhancing regional stability'. These were the official phrases used to describe the American arms build-up, which to the Soviet Union appeared to be preparation for war and perhaps for a first strike against strategic targets in the Soviet Far East. Not only did the Americans build ten Ohio-class submarines for deployment in the Pacific, each capable of destroying 192 cities, but they also put large numbers of F—15, F—16 and F/A18 fighters in Japan and Korea, and equipped B52G bombers of the Strategic Air Command in Guam with air-launched cruise missiles. 'Demonstrations of American resolve', as they were comfortingly called in Washington, were interpreted in Moscow as precursors to aggression, just as the Soviet Union's 'modernisation' program for its Far East nuclear forces in the decade before the war was evidence to the Americans that the nuclear balance in the region had shifted in favour of their enemy, and that the Russians were intent upon war in the Pacific. The arms race fed upon itself.

The bases, the ships, the aircraft and the troops were the most obvious parts of a far more complex machine for waging nuclear war. Less known, though equally vital, were facilities for what was called C^3I or 'command, control, communications and intelligence', that is, the brain functions of the war which was soon to come. If people could somehow have seen the American side of this vast system it would have emerged as a

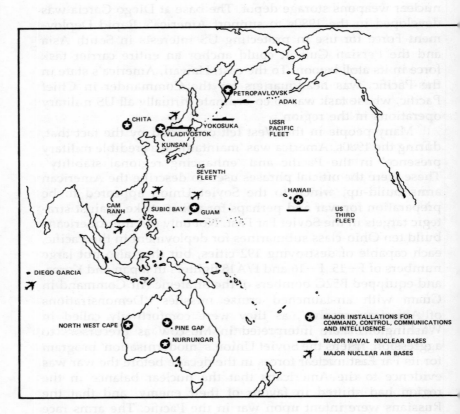

The Pacific Nuclear Web, Soviet and American. These bases and installation
are only the most obvious parts of a far more comprehensive network o
facilities and weapon systems confronting each other in the Pacific and Fa
East.

web of listening devices and electronic trip-wires on the earth, under the sea and in space. A web spread across the Pacific from the west coast of the USA to East Asia and Australia, each strand linked with the rest. A similar, though less sophisticated, Soviet web was centred upon signals intelligence bases and satellite ground stations at Chita and Petropavlovsk.

Finding out what the other side was doing became an obsession during the 1980s, and the USA in particular expended great resources on monitoring the movements of enemy forces, especially submarines. Hydrophones placed on the floor of the sea picked up the sounds of submarines and sent the information to the USA via satellite; ground stations of the US Navy's Ocean Surveillance Satellite System, given the name 'Classic Wizard', collected information in Guam, Diego Garcia (Indian Ocean) and Adak (Alaska); bases for the Defense Satellite Communications System and Fleet Satellite Communications relayed their intelligence to central posts for interpretation and analysis; and by the early 1990s the US Navy had built 12 special ships which towed long hydrophone equipment behind them to detect the sounds of Soviet submarines.

An increasingly intricate array of signals-intelligence stations intercepted millions of electronic communications every day, on both sides. Under an agreement which for long remained secret, the UKUSA Agreement or 'Secret Treaty' of 1947, the security and intelligence agencies of the USA, Australia, Britain, Canada and New Zealand co-operated in electronic interception. The SIGINT station at Tangimoana in New Zealand checked naval and air traffic in the South Pacific as far east as Latin America. Australia, because of its position on the globe, was especially valued by the USA as a site for satellite ground installations. At Pine Gap in central Australia the CIA ran a facility which, with its seven large radomes and vast computers, was linked to intelligence satellites over the Pacific; and the US Defense Support Program's station at Nurrungar in South Australia, like Pine Gap, was designed to give early warning of a Soviet missile attack by transmitting information from detection satellites. From Jim Creek (Washington State), North West Cape (Australia), Wahiawa (Hawaii) and Yosami (Japan) US Navy personnel sent messages to submerged nuclear submarines using very low frequency radio transmissions.

As the war showed, all these parts of the nuclear warfare brain were extremely vulnerable to attack. The war planners on both sides had correctly recognised that systems for anti-submarine warfare and C^3I were vital for the authorities to be able to know what was happening and to tell their officers what to do. But in the event, these electronic eyes and ears quickly disappeared, leaving the nuclear war machine to explode in uncontrolled fashion, like an ignited bag of fire-crackers. The war planners' vision proved to be true—the globe itself was their battlefield, with military facilities in numerous countries interlinked in a global network—but they had not foreseen how easily the links would be broken.

The arms race in the Pacific explains only in part why the Catastrophe began there. A second major reason is that the superpowers faced far fewer political restraints on the use of nuclear weapons in the Pacific than in Europe or the Middle East. The European peace protests of the early 1980s may not have prevented the deployment of a new generation of American missiles in answer to the Soviet SS–20s, but they alerted European governments to the risk of a nuclear war initiated by the superpowers on European territory. Those governments insisted upon either a dual-key arrangement which gave them a veto over the pressing of the button, or else a system of consultation with the Americans; in the eastern European countries of the Warsaw Pact similar agreements of a less binding kind seem to have been reached with Moscow, though these were not made public. Both superpowers thus possessed unwilling allies whose first priority was national survival. In the Middle East constant shifts in alliances and the evident risks of nuclear escalation from local conflicts bred caution on the part of the superpowers.

In the Pacific, allies applauded rather than criticised the superpowers. The American nuclear missiles stored at Kunsan in South Korea were under US control, and the South Korean government was in any case in favour of their use. As the US Army Chief of Staff in Korea, Edward Meyer, said in 1983 of the use of these weapons, 'It's far simpler here than in Europe, where consultations have to be made with 15 different sovereign nations'. The end of human life on the Korean Peninsula within a few days, as we now know, was the result of the 'simple' nuclear solution adopted on both sides of the De-militarised Zone. With the single exception of New Zealand, whose pleas for mediation went unheard in Washington and Moscow, American allies throughout the Pacific supported the defiant announcement by the US President that he would take 'whatever measures were necessary to defend freedom in the Philippines when freedom was under attack'.

The same pattern characterised Soviet use of nuclear weapons in Vietnam, which was the only country outside the USSR to carry Soviet nuclear weapons. The Vietnamese govern-ment, heavily reliant on the Soviet Union for economic aid and military assistance in its continuing war in Kampuchea, was as supine an ally on the Soviet side as South Korea was on the American, and in its few public statements before its obliteration it enthusiastically backed the Kremlin's determi-nation 'to defend the Socialist Revolution in the Philippines and the Soviet Motherland whatever the cost'. The Soviets made all the decisions about firing nuclear weapons. They began by firing an FRAS—1 anti-submarine rocket, fitted with a five kiloton nuclear depth charge—a small weapon by nuclear standards—but this soon escalated to the ship-to-ship miss-iles such as the Shaddock SS—N—3 carrying warheads with yields of about 250 kilotons, and by the end of the war, after 11 hours, they were launching SS—20s with three separate warheads of 600 kilotons each. Tokyo was obliterated by only one such warhead. Which side first crossed the nuclear frontier will never be known, but the idea that nuclear war could then be limited proved fatally wrong, as our damaged planet tes-tifies. Weapon after weapon, each more destructive than the last, was thrown into a battle which spread rapidly and engulfed most of the northern hemisphere within a day.

A third major reason for the Catastrophe lies in the politi-cal circumstances of the Pacific itself. The reckless misrule of the Philippines by Marcos ended in 1986 with a legacy of serious instability. After a honeymoon period in government the regime of Corazon Aquino, unable to solve the economic problems of the country, came under increasing pressure from the New People's Army to undertake genuine land reform. This it was unwilling to do, and the Communist insurgency grew rapidly as the landless and the unemployed flocked to join the revolution. Finally triumphant over a demoralised Philippine Army, the New People's Army came to power largely without ties to an overseas Communist patron. But the abortive CIA-inspired counter-revolution drove the revolutionary government into the waiting arms of the Soviet Union, which was eager to supply aid in return for the right to occupy the Subic and Clark bases. The US Navy and Air Force remained at Subic and Clark, American enclaves in a hostile country. To the Americans the nightmare of Castro's Cuba seemed to be repeating itself in the western Pacific, and the US government was determined upon a policy of staying put in the Philippines. Soviet control of the Philippine bases, Washington said, would alter the strategic balance throughout the Pacific. It could not be conceded.

The eruption of nuclear conflict in the Pacific illustrated the danger of two developments of the 1980s: the resurgence of an ignorant patriotism, and the nuclearisation of the seas. The sinking of two great ships at sea, the Soviet Kiev-class carrier *Lenin* and the USS *Carl Vinson*, affected public opinion more than other acts of war might have done. For a week after this clash the fate of the world hung in the balance. But patriotic feeling ran high, especially in the USA, where the government came under pressure to avenge the attack. Except in a few newspapers such as the *Washington Post* and the *New York Times*, leader writers demanded that the President should not let America be pushed around, and that this time the Russians had to be taught a lesson they would never forget. Interviewed on CBS news, the Commander in Chief Pacific, Admiral James J. Berghauser, called for America to use its nuclear capability to strike selected naval and land targets and to achieve a 'strategic environment favourable to the USA'. Half a century of Cold War propaganda in both the superpower states had the effect of making people think that a nuclear war could be fought, limited and won.

Escalation from conventional to nuclear weapons was far quicker than it would have been in a confrontation between forces on land such as those of NATO and the Warsaw Pact in Europe. Whereas the American National Command Authority possessed electronic means of controlling the firing of nuclear weapons by the Army and the Air Force, it had no way of preventing the unauthorised launch of nuclear missiles from submarines. Instead, the American President had to depend upon strict naval procedures which required a properly authenticated order before missiles could be released. Before the war the system seemed safe enough. Four officers had to cooperate in using keys and switches before a missile was fired from their submarine. But in the first hours of the final conflict, a number of submarines were too deeply submerged to receive very low frequency radio communications instructing them not to act, and at least two commanding officers apparently took the initiative in using nuclear weapons.

We need not dwell on the course of the war. So much happened so quickly that such an account would proceed by minutes rather than hours or days. But it should be said that the conflict confirmed the perceptiveness of the nineteenth century philosopher Carl von Clausewitz, whose classic treatise On War (1832) stressed the unpredictability of any recourse to arms by large bodies of men. In advance, Clausewitz said, everything looked simple and the strategic options appeared obvious; once war began, however, soldiers found that things constantly went wrong. The neat theories of war planners foundered on the reality of malfunctioning equipment, unexpected setbacks, poor communications and the need to make decisions in the field.

The electronic anonymity of the war compounded such problems. Within half an hour the satellite early warning system linked through stations in Guam and Australia to satellites over the Indian, Atlantic and Pacific Oceans had been destroyed, and the Soviet command centre at Petropavlovsk had been vaporised by Tomahawk cruise missiles. The Americans' 'Pacific Barrier' of radar stations in Guam, the Philippines and the Marshall Islands disappeared soon afterwards, along with much of the island of Oahu in Hawaii, the vital centre of the Americans' Pacific Command: one SS–20 with a 600 kiloton warhead turned Honolulu and Waikiki into ash. In this manner gaping holes were torn in the intricate web of facilities for control, command, communications and intelligence, and although a few aircraft on both sides survived as airborne command posts their officers were left with nothing to command. With the destruction of Chita in the fourth hour the Russians also lost central control of the nuclear battle, which degenerated into a series of independent nuclear exchanges. Men in charge of nuclear weapons, cut off from their superiors and acting in panic, ordered more and more attacks on enemy targets.

One tenth of the enormous firepower of the superpower arsenals in the Far East and the Pacific was enough to destroy the region utterly.

Endnotes

1 Where to test?

1 Walter LaFeber *America, Russia and the Cold War 1945–1966,* New York: John Wiley & Sons, 1967, p.21
2 ibid. p.35
3 Michael Mandelbaum *The Nuclear Question: The United States and Nuclear Weapons, 1946–1976* Cambridge: Cambridge University Press, 1979, p.19
4 U.S. Joint Task Force One *Bombs at Bikini: the official report of Operation Crossroads, prepared under the direction of the Commander of Joint Task Force One, by W.A. Shurcliff, historian of Joint Task Force One* New York: W.H. Wise, 1947, pp.2–3
5 David Bradley *No Place to Hide 1946/1984* Hanover: University Press of New England, 1983, p.55
6 ibid. pp.44, 95
7 Neal O. Hines *Proving Ground; an account of the radiobiological studies in the Pacific 1946–1961* Seattle: University of Washington Press, 1962, pp.45,51
8 ibid. p.76
9 ibid. p.78
10 Dorothy E. Richard *United States Naval Administration of the Trust Territory of the Pacific Islands* The Wartime Military Government Period vol.1, Washington D.C., 1957, p.160
11 Hines *Proving Ground* p.144
12 *The Report of the Royal Commission into British Nuclear Tests in Australia* Canberra: Australian Government Publishing Service, 1985, p.405
13 ibid., p.11
14 ibid., p.15
15 Denys Blakeway and Sue Lloyd-Roberts *Fields of Thunder. Testing Britain's Bomb* London: Unwin Paperbacks, 1985, p.73
16 Chapman Pincher *Inside Story. A Documentary of the Pursuit of Power* London: Sidgwick and Jackson, 1978, p.179
17 Blakeway and Lloyd-Roberts *Fields of Thunder,* p.160
18 Alfred Grosser *French Foreign Policy under de Gaulle* Boston: Little Brown & Co, 1967, p.107

19   Ministère des affaires étrangères *White Paper on the French nuclear tests* Paris, 1973, p.5
20   Ministry of Foreign Affairs *French Nuclear Testing in the Pacific. International Court of Justice. Nuclear Tests Case, New Zealand v. France*, vol.1, Wellington, 1973, p.42

2   Bravo
1   Robert A. Divine *Blowing on the Wind. The Nuclear Test Ban Debate 1954–1960* New York: Oxford University Press, 1978, p.3
2   Norman Moss *Men Who Play God. The Story of the Hydrogen Bomb* London: Victor Gollancz, 1968, p.86
3   Fifth Congress of Micronesia, First Regular Session *A Report on the People of Rongelap and Utirik Relative to Medical Aspects of the March 1, 1954 Incident. Injury, Examination and Treatment* Saipan, 1973, p.80
4   *Marshall Islands Journal* 17 May 1985
5   *A Report on the People*, p.141
6   Divine *Blowing on the Wind*, pp.27–9
7   Defense Nuclear Agency *Castle Series 1954* Washington, Apr. 1982, pp.3, 235
8   Divine *Blowing on the Wind*, pp.8–25
9   Y. Kondo, K. Fujita and H. Ogura 'Economic Aspects of Effects of Bikini H-Bomb experiments on Japanese Fisheries' in *Research in the Effects and Influences of the Nuclear Bomb Test Explosions* vol.2, Tokyo: Japan Society for the Promotion of Science, 1956, p.1279
10   US Atomic Energy Commission *The Effects of High-Yield Nuclear Explosions* Feb. 1955
11   Divine *Blowing on the Wind*, p.57
12   Defense Nuclear Agency *Operation Hardtack I 1958* Washington D.C., 1982
13   Glenn T. Seaborg *Kennedy, Krushchev and the Test Ban* Berkeley: University of California Press, 1981, pp.156–7

3   Unto the Promised Land
1   Quoted in Robert C. Kiste *The Bikinians: A Study in Forced Migration* Menlo Park, California: Cummings Publishing Co., 1974, p.28
2   David Bradley *No Place to Hide, 1946/1984*, Hanover: University Press of New England, 1983, pp.162–3
3   Kiste *The Bikinians* p.110
4   Robert C. Kiste 'The Relocation of the Bikini Marshallese' in Michael D. Lieber (ed.) *Exiles and Migrants in Oceania* Honolulu: The University Press of Hawaii, 1977, pp.99–100
5   Kiste *The Bikinians* p.147
6   *The Washington Post* 19 Mar. 1978
7   *The Washington Post* 13 Apr. and 22 May 1978
8   US Department of Energy *Radiological Survey Plan for the Northern Marshall Islands* 1978, p.ii–3
9   *Marshall Islands Journal* 26 Apr. and 23 Aug. 1985

10   *Radiological Survey Plan* p.ii—3
11   Jack Tobin 'The Resettlement of the Enewetak People: a Study of a Displaced Community in the Marshall Islands' PhD dissertation, University of California, Berkeley, 1967, pp.42—3
12   ibid. p.230
13   Eluklab was vaporised on 1 Nov. 1952, Dridrilbwij on 23 May 1958. Holmes and Narver Inc. *Cleanup, rehabilitation, resettlement of Enewetak Atoll, Marshall Islands: environmental impact statement,* vol.1, Washington: Defense Nuclear Agency, 1975, p.3/49
14   Department of the Air Force *Draft Environmental Statement. Pacific Cratering Experiments (PACE)* Feb. 1973, p.1/38
15   Quoted in Robert C. Kiste 'The People of Enewetak Atoll vs the US Department of Defense', Pacific Collection, Hamilton Library, University of Hawaii, n.d., p.13
16   Holmes and Narver *Cleanup,* p.5/1—5
17   Floyd K. Takeuchi 'Enewetak. A Nuclear Legacy' *Glimpses of Micronesia & the Western Pacific* 20, 3, 1980, pp.32—7
18   *Marshall Islands Gazette* 21 Mar. 1983
19   *Marshall Islands Journal* 24 May 1985
20   US General Accounting Office *Enewetak Atoll-Cleaning Up Nuclear Contamination* 8 May 1979, p.15

4   'It turns out we were wrong'
1   See David Robie *Eyes of Fire. The Last Voyage of the Rainbow Warrior* Auckland: Lindon Publishing, 1986, pp.47—77
2   *Marshall Islands Journal* 31 May 1985
3   Neal O. Hines *Proving Ground; an account of the radiobiological studies in the Pacific 1946—1961* Seattle: University of Washington Press, 1962, p.218
4   ibid. p.238
5   Fifth Congress of Micronesia, First Regular Session, *A Report on the People of Rongelap and Utirik Relative to Medical Aspects of the March 1, 1954 Incident. Injury, Examination and Treatment* Saipan, 1973, p.102
6   UN Trusteeship Council *UN Visiting Mission to the Trust Territories of Nauru, New Guinea and the Pacific Islands, 1959. Report on the Trust Territory of the Pacific Islands,* pp.19—20
7   UN Trusteeship Council *Report of the UN Visiting Mission to the Trust Territory of the Pacific Islands, 1961,* pp.89—93
8   *A Report on the People* p.109
9   *UN Visiting Mission 1959,* p.20
10   Robert A. Conard and others *Review of Medical Findings in a Marshallese Population 26 Years After Accidental Exposure to Radioactive Fallout* Upton, NY: Brookhaven National Laboratory, 1980, pp.59, 74—6, 81
11   ibid. p.86
12   Quoted in *A Report on the People,* p.151
13   Giff Johnson *Collision Course at Kwajalein. Marshall Islanders in the*

Shadow of the Bomb Honolulu: Pacific Concerns Resource Center, 1984, p.14

14 *Micronesian Independent* 24 June 1977
15 Conard to John R. Totter, 9 Apr. 1969 (copy in possession of author)
16 World Council of Churches *Marshall Islands: 37 years after. Report of a World Council of Churches Delegation to the Marshall Islands 20 May−4 June 1983* Geneva: WCC, 1983, pp.31−2, 37
17 Glenn Alcalay 'Maelstrom in the Marshall Islands: The Social Impact of Nuclear Weapons Testing' in Catherine Lutz (ed.) *Micronesia as Strategic Colony. The Impact of US policy on Micronesian Health and Culture* Cambridge, Mass: Cultural Survival Inc, 1984, p.36
18 98th Congress, 2nd Session *Hearing before the Subcommittee on Public Lands and National Parks of the Committee on Interior and Insular Affairs House of Representatives on Section 177 of the Proposed Compact of Free Association: Compensation for Victims of US Nuclear Testing in the Marshall Islands* 8 May 1984, 98−56, II, p.54
19 ibid. p.272
20 Jonathan M. Weisgall 'Micronesia and the Nuclear Pacific since Hiroshima', *SAIS Review* 5, 2, 1985, p.50
21 98th Congress *Hearing on Section 177*, p.49

5 Staying while leaving

1 Quoted in John C. Dorrance 'Micronesian Crosscurrents and the US Role in the Western Pacific. A Case Study of US Interests, Objectives and Policy Implementation with Recommendations for Change' dissertation, National War College, Washington, 1975, p.37
2 R.H. Wyttenbach 'Micronesia and Strategic Trusteeship: a case study in American Politico-Military Relations' PhD dissertation, Fletcher School of Law and Diplomacy, Mass., 1971, pp.viii−ix
3 Dorrance 'Micronesian Crosscurrents', pp.38−9
4 98th Congress, 2nd Session *Hearings before the Subcommittee on Public Lands and National Parks of the Committee on Interior and Insular Affairs House of Representatives on the National Security Implications of the Compact of Free Association* 7 and 9 Aug. 1984, 98−56, VI, p.1
5 Administration to Senate Committee on Energy and Natural Resources, 27 Jan. 1982, in *Hearing before the Committee on Energy and Natural Resources United States Senate on S.J. Res. 286* 24 May 1984
6 US *Congressional Record* 25 July 1985, 131, 101, p.H6330
7 ibid. p.H6341
8 ibid. p.H6343
9 Henry Schwalbenberg 'American Military Needs in Micronesia: Valid Perceptions or Unnecessary Contingencies?' Truk: Micronesian Seminar, 1982, p.2
10 UN Department of Political Affairs, Trusteeship and Decolonization *Decolonization* 16, 1980, p.49

6 Islands with a military future

1 *Rengel Belau* 2−16 Sept. 1984

2 Roger Clark and Sue Rabbitt Roff *Micronesia: The Problem of Palau* New York: Minority Rights Group Report No 63, 1984, pp.14–15
3 *Rengel Belau* 5–25 July and 5–18 Aug. 1984
4 KLTAL-RENG/Belau Pacific Center *Belau Plebiscite 1984: an independent report* Koror, 1984.
5 Petition Concerning the Trust Territory of the Pacific Islands Presented to the United Nations Trusteeship Council on behalf of the International League for Human Rights by Roger S. Clark, 13 May 1986
6 USIA Wireless File, East Asia Pacific, 24 Feb. 1986
7 Information from Charles Scheiner, 15 July 1986
8 John C. Dorrance 'United States Security Interests in the Pacific Islands' *World Review* 23, 1, 1984, p.11
9 US *Senate Hearing on S.J. Res. 286* 24 May 1984, pp.896–7
10 US *House Hearings on Compact* 7 and 9 Aug. 1984, p.27
11 ibid. p.29
12 *Marshall Islands Journal* 25 Aug. 1982
13 *New York Times* 13 Sept. 1982
14 *Marshall Islands Journal* 9 Sept. 1982
15 Henry Schwalbenberg 'Marshallese Political Developments: No to Commonwealth' Truk: Micronesian Seminar, 1984, p.2
16 *Sydney Morning Herald* 8 May 1986
17 Kwajalein Atoll Corporation to House Subcommittee on Public Lands and National Parks,1 Mar. 1985, in *House Hearings on Compact* 7 and 9 Aug. 1984, p.34

7 'Where Aboriginals could not be'

1 *The Report of the Royal Commission into British Nuclear Tests in Australia* Canberra: Australian Government Publishing Service, 1985, p.118

2 ibid. p.450
3 ibid. p.477
4 ibid. pp.172–3
5 ibid. p.177
6 ibid. pp.174–6
7 ibid. pp.146–7
8 ibid. p.300
9 ibid. p.303
10 ibid. p.374
11 ibid. pp.308–9
12 ibid. p.316
13 ibid. pp.318–9
14 ibid. p.376
15 ibid. p.379
16 ibid. p.378
17 Adrian Tame and F.P.J. Robotham *Maralinga. British A–Bomb, Australian Legacy* Melbourne: Fontana Books, 1982, p.141. See also

Robert Milliken *No Conceivable Injury* Ringwood: Penguin Books (Australia), 1986, pp.111–17

18 *Royal Commission*, p.321
19 ibid. p.322
20 ibid. p.405
21 *The Report of the Royal Commission into British Nuclear Tests in Australia. Conclusions and Recommendations* Canberra: Australian Government Publishing Service, 1985, p.31
22 *Sydney Morning Herald* 23 Jan. 1986
23 Denys Blakeway and Sue Lloyd-Roberts *Fields of Thunder. Testing Britain's Bomb* London: Unwin Paperbacks, 1985, p.175
24 Eric Bailey *The Christmas Island Story* London: Stacey International, 1977, p.61

8 Raison d'état

1 This chapter is based on accounts published in the *Age*, the *Australian*, *Greenpeace Examiner*, the *Guardian Weekly*, the *Honolulu Star-Bulletin*, *Islands Business*, *Le Monde*, the *Sydney Morning Herald* and *Time*. I also used cables from Reuter, Australian Associated Press, the New York Times News Service and Agence France Presse.

See Richard Shears and Isobelle Gidley *The Rainbow Warrior Affair* Sydney: Unwin Paperbacks, 1985; John Dyson *Sink the Rainbow! An enquiry into the 'Greenpeace Affair'* Auckland: Reed Methuen, 1986; the Sunday Times Insight Team *Rainbow Warrior* London: Arrow Books, 1986; and David Robie *Eyes of Fire. The Last Voyage of the Rainbow Warrior* Auckland: Lindon Publishing, 1986.

9 Moruroa

1 *Guardian Weekly* 13 Apr. 1986
2 Bengt Danielsson and Marie-Thérèse Danielsson *Poisoned Reign. French nuclear colonialism in the Pacific* Ringwood: Penguin Books (Australia), 1986, p.63
3 ibid. p.100
4 Philippe Mazellier *Tahiti de l'atome à l'autonomie* Papeete, 1979, p.212
5 NZ Ministry of Foreign Affairs *French Nuclear Testing* vol.1, p.31
6 International Court of Justice *Pleadings, Oral Arguments, Documents. Nuclear Tests Cases, New Zealand v. France*, vol.2, The Hague, 1978, pp.110, 114
7 ibid. *Australia v. France* vol.1, The Hague, 1978, pp.169, 180
8 David McTaggart *Greenpeace III. Journey into the Bomb* London: Collins, 1978, p.274
9 ibid. p.280
10 Greenpeace New Zealand *French Polynesia The Nuclear Tests: a chronology 1967–1981* Auckland, 1981
11 Danielssons *Poisoned Reign* p.215
12 *ACFOA Research and Information Service* June 1982, p.2
13 'Broadband' 28 Nov. 1979
14 *Nation Review* Mar. 1980, p.18

15 The French Army map is reproduced in *Pacific Islands Monthly* Aug. 1983, p.35
16 *Pacific Islands Monthly* Oct. 1981, p.23
17 ibid. June 1983, pp.31–2
18 *Report of a New Zealand, Australian and Papua-New Guinea Scientific Mission to Mururoa Atoll* Wellington, 1984
19 Paris speech by Mitterrand, 15 Sep. 1986, Reuter.
20 *Report of a ... Mission to Mururoa* p.106
21 *Islands Business* Sep. 1985, p.28
22 *Canberra Times* 22 Feb. 1986
23 Jacqui Drollet 'Passing Governments and Permanent Geopolitics in Today's Pacific', paper to the UN University Conference, Auckland, Apr. 1986, p.1

10 Why the French love the bomb

1 Pierre Mauroy, speech, 20 Sep. 1982
2 International Court of Justice, *Pleadings, Oral Arguments, Documents. Nuclear Test Cases, Australia v. France*, vol.1, The Hague, 1978, p.28
3 *Pacific News* July/Aug. 1986, pp.3–4. See also Martyn Lyons *The Totem and the Tricolour: A Short History of New Caledonia since 1774* Kensington, NSW: New South Wales University Press, 1986
4 Quoted in Robbin F. Laird 'French Nuclear Forces in the 1980s and the 1990s' *Comparative Strategy* 4, 4, 1984, p.395
5 ibid. p.400
6 *Sydney Morning Herald* 14 Nov. 1985
7 Tony Chafer 'Politics and the Perception of Risk: A Study of the Anti-Nuclear Movements in Britain and France' *West European Politics* 8, 1, 1985, p.13
8 Quoted in Denis MacShane *François Mitterrand: A Political Odyssey* London: Quartet Books, 1982, pp.115–16
9 Diana Johnstone 'How the French Left Learned to Love the Bomb' *New Left Review* 146, 1984, p.8
10 *Guardian Weekly* 15 Sep. 1985
11 John Ralston Saul 'The malaise that threatens France' *The Spectator* 5 Oct. 1985, p.9
12 *Guardian Weekly* 14 Oct. 1985
13 *Canberra Times* 4 Jan. 1986
14 *Sydney Morning Herald* 1 Feb. 1986

11 Crisis in ANZUS

1 *Australian Financial Review* 7 Feb. 1985
2 *New Zealand Herald* 11 Sep. 1985; F.A. Mediansky 'Nuclear Weapons and Security in the South Pacific' *The Washington Quarterly* Winter 1986, p.33
3 *New York Times* 29 Sep. 1985
4 *New Zealand Herald* 16 Sep. 1985
5 *New York Times* 6 Oct. 1985
6 *New Zealand Herald* 18 Jan. 1986

7 John C. Dorrance 'ANZUS: Misperceptions, Mythology and Reality', Aug. 1985, p.17
8 Australia, Department of Foreign Affairs *Backgrounder* 29 Feb. 1984
9 *Australian Foreign Affairs Record* June 1984, pp.618–19
10 ibid. Apr. 1984, p.307
11 Murray Goot and Peter King 'ANZUS Reconsidered: the Domestic Politics of an Alliance' in J. Bercovitch (ed.) *ANZUS in Crisis: Alliance Management in International Affairs* London: Macmillan (forthcoming)
12 *Backgrounder* 27 Feb. 1985
13 *Sydney Morning Herald* 28 June and 13 Aug. 1986
14 ibid. 7 June 1986
15 ibid. 17 Dec. 1986
16 Mediansky 'Nuclear Weapons' p.42
17 John C. Dorrance 'United States Security Interests in the Pacific Islands,' *World Review* 23, 1, 1984, p.14
18 *Pacific Islands Monthly* Dec. 1984, p.15
19 *The National Times* 25 Apr.–1 May 1986, p.5
20 F. Rawdon Dalrymple 'Partners, Friends and Allies: Australia and the Pacific' 24 Sep. 1985
21 *Sydney Morning Herald* 17 Mar. 1986

12 Becoming nuclear free
1 Vijay Naidu 'The Fiji Anti-Nuclear Movement: Problems and Prospects', paper to the UN University Conference, Auckland, Apr. 1986, p.5
2 World Council of Churches *Marshall Islands: 37 years after* Report of a World Council of Churches Delegation to the Marshall Islands 20 May–4 June 1983, Geneva: WCC, 1983, pp.19, 37, 44
3 *Sydney Morning Herald* 17 May 1986; *Washington Pacific Report* 1 June 1986
4 Nuclear Free and Independent Pacific Conference—1983, July 10–20, 1983, Port Vila, Vanuatu, p.27
5 ibid. p.11
6 Greg Fry 'Australia, New Zealand and Arms Control in the Pacific Region' in Desmond Ball (ed.) *The Anzac Connection* Sydney: George Allen & Unwin, 1985, pp.91–118
7 *Report by the Chairman of the Working Group on a South Pacific Nuclear Free Zone to the South Pacific Forum Rarotonga 4–6 Aug. 1985*, p.5
8 *South Pacific Nuclear Free Zone Treaty and Draft Protocols Adopted at Rarotonga, 6 Aug. 1985* Wellington: August 1985
9 *Pacific News* July/Aug. 1985, pp.1, 5–9
10 Quoted in Ball *Anzac Connection*, pp.108–9
11 *Pacific Islands Monthly* Feb. 1985, p.46
12 ibid. May 1986, p.16
13 *New Zealand Herald* 6 Jan. 1986
14 *Australian Financial Review* 4 Aug. 1986

15 Gwyn Prins (ed.) *The Choice: Nuclear Weapons versus Security* London: Chatto and Windus, 1984, p.24
16 Helen Clark 'Alliances and Nuclear Politics', speech to the Sixth Annual Forum of Parliamentarians for World Order, New York, 30 Oct. 1985
17 William M. Arkin and Richard W. Fieldhouse *Nuclear Battlefields. Global Links in the Arms Race* Cambridge, Mass: Ballinger Publishing Company, 1985, p.128
18 Speech to Conference on Disarmament, Geneva, 7 Aug. 1984, *Backgrounder* 8 Aug. 1984, p.A16
19 George F. Kennan *The Nuclear Delusion. Soviet-American Relations in the Atomic Age* New York: Pantheon Books, 1982, pp.194—5

13 Epilogue

In writing this imaginary history of the origins of World War III, I drew upon a variety of sources, of which the most useful were: William M. Arkin and Richard W. Fieldhouse *Nuclear Battlefields. Global Links in the Arms Race* Cambridge, Mass: Ballinger Publishing Company, 1985; Jeffrey T. Richelson and Desmond Ball *The Ties That Bind* Boston: Allen & Unwin, 1985; Desmond Ball 'Nuclear War at Sea', *International Security* 10, 3, 1985—86, pp.3—31; Donald C. Daniel and Gael D. Tarleton 'The US Navy in the Western Pacific: The View from the Mid-1980s', *USA Today* May 1985, pp.11—20; Peter Hayes, Lyuba Zarsky and Walden Bello *American Lake. Nuclear Peril in the Pacific* Ringwood: Penguin Books (Australia), 1986, and earlier manuscript versions of this book.

Bibliography

Arkin, William M. and Fieldhouse, Richard W. *Nuclear Battlefields. Global Links in the Arms Race* Cambridge, Mass: Ballinger Publishing Company, 1985

Ball, Desmond (ed.) *The Anzac Connection* Sydney: George Allen & Unwin, 1985

Bertell, Rosalie *No Immediate Danger. Prognosis for a Radioactive Earth* London: The Women's Press, 1985

Blakeway, Denys and Lloyd-Roberts, Sue *Fields of Thunder. Testing Britain's Bomb* London: Unwin Paperbacks, 1985

Bradley, David *No Place to Hide 1946/1984* Hanover: University Press of New England, 1983

Cockburn, Stewart and Ellyard, David *Oliphant* Adelaide: Axiom Books, 1981

Danielsson, Bengt and Danielsson, Marie-Thérèse *Poisoned Reign. French nuclear colonialism in the Pacific* Ringwood: Penguin Books (Australia), 1986

Divine, Robert A. *Blowing on the Wind. The Nuclear Test Ban Debate 1954–1960* New York: Oxford University Press, 1978

Dyson, John *Sink the Rainbow! An enquiry into the 'Greenpeace Affair'* Auckland: Reed Methuen, 1986

Gold, Hyam *New Directions in New Zealand Foreign Policy* Auckland: Benton Ross, 1985

Hayes, Peter, Zarsky, Lyuba and Bello, Walden, *American Lake, Nuclear Peril in the Pacific* Ringwood: Penguin Books (Australia), 1986

Hines, Neal O. *Proving Ground: an account of the radiobiological studies in the Pacific 1946–1961* Seattle: University of Washington Press, 1962

Johnson, Giff *Collision Course at Kwajalein. Marshall Islanders in the Shadow of the Bomb* Honolulu: Pacific Concerns Resource Center, 1984

Kiste, Robert C. *The Bikinians* Menlo Park, Calif.: Cummings Publishing Company, 1974

Lutz, Catherine (ed.) *Micronesia as Strategic Colony. The Impact of U.S. Policy on Micronesian Health and Culture* Cambridge, Mass: Cultural Survival Inc., 1984

Lyons, Martyn *The Totem and the Tricolour. A Short History of New*

Caledonia since 1774 Kensington, NSW: New South Wales University Press, 1986

McTaggart, David *Greenpeace III. Journey into the Bomb* London: Collins, 1978

Milliken, Robert *No Conceivable Injury. The story of Britain and Australia's atomic cover-up* Ringwood: Penguin Books (Australia), 1986

Pacific News Bulletin Nuclear Free & Independent Pacific Coordinating Committee, Sydney, 1986—

Phillips, Dennis H. *Cold War Two and Australia* Sydney: George Allen & Unwin, 1983

The Report of the Royal Commission into British Nuclear Tests in Australia 2 vols, Canberra: Australian Government Publishing Service, 1985

Richelson, Jeffrey and Ball, Desmond *The Ties That Bind. Intelligence Cooperation Between the UKUSA Countries—the United Kingdom, the United States of America, Canada, Australia and New Zealand* Boston: Allen & Unwin, 1985

Robie, David *Eyes of Fire. The Last Voyage of the Rainbow Warrior* Auckland: Lindon Publishing, 1986

Shears, Richard and Gidley, Isobelle *The Rainbow Warrior Affair* Sydney: Unwin Paperbacks, 1985

The Sunday Times Insight Team *Rainbow Warrior. The French attempt to sink Greenpeace* London: Arrow books, 1986

Symonds, J.L. *A History of British Atomic Tests in Australia* Canberra: Australian Government Publishing Service, 1985

Tame, Adrian and F.P.J. Robotham *Maralinga. British A-Bomb, Australian Legacy* Australia: Fontana Books, 1982

Thakur, Ramesh *In Defence of New Zealand; Foreign Policy Choices in the Nuclear Age* Wellington: New Zealand Institute of International Affairs, 1984

World Council of Churches *Marshall Islands: 37 years after* Geneva: WWC, 1983

Index